*Face It —
Trace It —
Erase It!*

Life Beyond Fear
Living without Limits

Nate Holcomb

Unless otherwise indicated, all Scripture quotations are from the King James Version of the Bible.

Life Beyond Fear
Living without Limits
ISBN: 978-0-9850558-2-0
1st Printing
Copyright © 2012 by Nathaniel Holcomb
IT'S ALL ABOUT HIM PUBLISHING
P. O. Box 1006
Copperas Cove, TX 76522

Printed in the United States of America by IT'S ALL ABOUT HIM PUBLISHING. All rights reserved under International Copyright Law. Contents and/or cover may not be reproduced in whole or in part in any form without express written consent of the publisher.

Acknowledgements

Many times I have claimed kinship to Moses, God's servant-leader of the great exodus. During his time, he needed Caleb, Joshua, and ten other leaders to assist in the mission set before him. Likewise, God has been extremely generous, and given me people for my life. He has surrounded me with many anointed and talented people.

As it pertains to "Life Beyond Fear," He has made no exception. Therefore, I want to take this opportunity to express my gratitude to those who assisted in the work. To my son, Tyrone Holcomb, who is a capable and extraordinary writer in his own right – thanks for overseeing this project, and for putting your heart into this assignment, because you knew how important it was and is to me. I am thankful for you, not only as your father, but as your pastor, also.

Thanks to you and the team:
Tyrone Holcomb – Compiler, Chief Editor, & Page Designer
Ramona Johnson – Editor
Olga Wise – Transcriptionist
Colathia Fay Walker – Cover/Book Designer

Life beyond Fear is a dimension designed by God where we can live, and experience living without limits!

Contents

1. Overcoming Fear by Faith...10
2. Overcoming the Fear of Death...16
3. Is There Pain In Death?...23
4. Overcoming the Fear of People..32
5. Overcoming the Fear of Rejection......................................41
6. Learning to Say No..49
7. Overcoming the Fear of Failure..58
8. The Trapeze Act...66
9. Overcoming the Fear of the Lion.......................................74
   Backtalk the Devil
10. Fix Your Heart..83
11. Overcoming the Fear of the Serpent.................................92
12. Get the Picture..99
13. Overcoming the Fear of the Dragon...............................107
    Addressing the Spirit of Paranoia
14. Eliminating the Spirit of Paranoia...................................116
15. The Disrespect of Fear..125

Introduction

Have you ever thought about what your life would be if the limitations were removed? Have you considered that many of those limitations just might be self-imposed because of a fear of failing, or fear of people, or the fear of being rejected?

Fear is a thief and a robber, taking by stealth or by force the pricelessness of confidence. The polar opposite of faith, fear keeps you from reaching too far or from accomplishing too much. In fact, fear is faith perverted and misplaced. Though they are governed by the same principles, faith's confidence rests in God, while fear trusts in the inevitability of the worst possible outcome. This pessimism is not innate, because no one is born with it. The sad commentary is you and I have been taught as children to be fearful, and the cycle is perpetuated, passed down to posterity.

But it is in your hands to halt its ravishing effects on your life. Even when surrounded by fearful circumstances, or spooked by imagined fears like the infamous boogeyman, you don't have to be governed by them. You can be delivered from them. On your journey through this book you will learn to obliterate the fears that have long plagued you, facing them, tracing them, erasing them, and replacing them with faith. You will remove apprehension from the helm of your life-ship, and set your course for the shores of abundant living.

Some will hear that and say, "If that's what you believe, then you haven't experienced life." Which life are they talking about? There are two types of life: life in the world and the Zoe (God-kind) of life. The world's life will reinforce your fears; but Zoe will deliver you from all your fears! Zoe-life will call fear out, like God did Adam in the Garden of Eden—"Who told you that?!" Zoe-life will answer fear's "cannots" with, "I can do all things through Christ who strengthens me!" It'll answer fear's "what ifs" with "If God is for me who can be against me and succeed?!"

The world will limit you, counting on fear to stop you from reaching too far; but God's Zoe-life will tell you that what God has prepared for you is far beyond what you can ask or think. Fear is grabbed by its collar and cast out of doors in God's presence; and thus there are no limits on you.

It is the Father's desire to restore the childlikeness of faith to His children because when it is present, fear is powerless and trust is at optimum levels. It starts with opening your heart to the possibility of moving into an unrestricted life, filled with potential, unabated by fear. Are you ready for this journey?

Part One

*O magnify the L*ORD *with me, and let us exalt his name together. I sought the L*ORD*, and he heard me, and delivered me from all my fears.*
Psalm 34:3-4 kjv

Chapter One

Overcoming Fear by Faith

> For whatsoever is born of God overcometh the world: and **this is the victory that overcometh the world, even our faith.**
> —1st John 5:4

Some never marry because they fear divorce. Others never start their business because they fear failing. No matter the positives in life many still fear the negatives. This kind of mind-set can create a lifeless existence. However, God desires the best for us. Therefore, He sent forth Jesus to liberate us from all our fears.

It Takes Faith to Move fear

Living without fear is possible! I realize such a statement can catch many off guard. However, a fearless life is not a statement it is a standard. As Christians we are to live life free from the bondage of fear. The only way to accomplish this is through a life of faith. In our everyday activities we are encouraged to walk by faith and not by what we see happening around us (2nd Co. 5:7). We are instructed through the Word of God to live by faith (Ro. 1:17).

Through faith we accomplish our God-given desires and without it we stifle our endeavors. Remember doubt neutralizes us, fear paralyzes us, unbelief sterilizes us, and faith energizes us. Faith will always move us from where we are to where God wants us. Whenever I need to go somewhere unfamiliar I use the GPS (Global Positioning System) in my car. Before imputing my destination, I must record my location. Once the device registers my current location it can direct me anywhere.

In like manner, the Lord desires to take us to greater heights in life. To do so we must use our spiritual GPS (God's Positioning System). God knows our location. Nevertheless, He needs us to know where we are in order to experience the quality life He's designed for us. Do you know where you are? More importantly, are you living in faith? If you are not living in faith you are living in fear, there's no two ways about it.

I once read a Peanut comic strip where Charlie Brown and Lucy were on a cruise ship. Lucy decided to take the opportunity and teach Charlie Brown a message of life. While on the deck of the ship, Lucy commented, "Look Charlie, some people placed their deck chairs at the back of the ship so they can see where they've been. And others placed their chairs in front of the ship in order to see where they're going. Many placed their chairs in the middle of the ship to show their happiness with where they are."

While speaking, Lucy noticed a puzzled look on Charlie Brown's face so she asked, "What's wrong Chuck?" To this he replied, "Gee Lucy, I'm just trying to get my deck chair unfolded." Without faith you'll be stuck in life trying to get your deck chair unfolded. Do not allow doubt to neutralize you or even worse—fear to paralyze you. Place your trust in God and allow faith to energize you.

The Father's Love Empowers Faith

Removing fear from our lives does not erase it altogether. Unfortunately, fear remains in this world. However, the presence of fear doesn't grant it power. Faith will always move us beyond fear.

II Timothy 1:7 tells us God has not given us the spirit of fear because He has given us power, love and a sound mind. We can clearly see from the aforementioned passage fear is a spirit. To possess a spirit of fear is considered a state of being. Just as sure as I live in the State of Texas within the United States of America, too many of God's people live in the state of fear. Yet this spirit is rendered powerless when we focus on the Father's love.

If we allow fear to dominate our lives we'll continue in that state and come short of God's victory and the experience of His love.

> Where God's love is, there is no fear, because God's perfect love drives out fear...
>
> —1st John 4:18 ncv

We must replace our fear with faith, which is strengthened through the Father's love. The devil fights to keep us ignorant, uneducated, and lacking power. However, because of His love, we are empowered.

Remember, the devil gains strength through our guilt. Guilt stems from sins, transgressions and iniquities. When Jesus bore our sins on the cross of Calvary, we were no longer guilty but recipients of the gift of His love. It was love that provoked Jesus to sacrifice His life for our offense then. And it is His love that empowers us today. *Jesus' love empowers us!*

People who experience a faith failure only reveal their inability to comprehend and appreciate the Father's love which empowers faith. His love never fails and neither should our faith.

An understanding of the Father's love compels us to operate by faith in that love. The Bible tells us faith works by love (Ga. 5:6). Allow me to share the following illustration to amplify the effects of the Father's love.

One evening a father and his young son was storing furniture in their cellar. The floor of their front porch had a doorway that allowed entry into the cellar. The father who was submerged into the cellar received the furniture from his son who stood atop the porch.

Suddenly the neighborhood experienced a blackout. In fear, the little boy began weeping because of the darkness. The father looking up at his son began to speak. "Son you need not be afraid, I'm right here." The son unable to see his father in the dark cellar cried out, "Daddy, I hear your voice, but I cannot see you."

The father looking to reassure his son said, "Son, remember how much I love you. I will never fail you." "I know you love me daddy," the son responded. Again the father reassured him, "Son, if you know I love you take one step and you will fall into my arms." Fearfully the boy answered, "Daddy I can't see you!"

The father reasoned, "It's not important for you to see me because I can see you clearly. Son if you know I love you, trust me and take the step." The little boy took the step because he had faith in his father's love. Beloved, perfect love cast out fear.

As Christians we are instructed to walk by faith. Even still, some are afraid to take the step because they can't determine the outcome. Remember, it doesn't matter what the future holds when you know Who holds your future. God has the whole world in His hands. He sees perfectly and He wants us to have faith in His love.

✴ Having faith in the Father's love empowers us to successfully live a life beyond fear.

THE FUNDAMENTALS OF FAITH

Faith has a fundamental principle. In short, this principle states God rewards those who trust in Him (Heb. 11:6). Not trusting God limits His power to perform in our lives (Ps. 78:41).

Let's consider a case where fear is pacified. Note, when fear is pacified faith is powerless. There is a child who is crying out of fear because he sees a puppy nearby. Wanting to calm the situation a man runs and picks up the child. This course of action has just pacified the child's fear of the puppy. However, if the man picks up the puppy in the presence of the child and plays with the puppy, he will destroy the child's fear of the pup. In essence, the child's fear is not confirmed. The child witnesses no harm from the puppy. And, the child's faith to play with the pup (or at least remain in the same room) will be empowered.

In this world the faithful may not live forever, but the fearful will not live at all. This is to say; one day we all must leave this life. Albeit, the faithful will have experienced a quality life and those who were fearful will have missed the victorious life God desired for them.

The Bible admonishes us to examine ourselves in order to remain in faith. Measuring whether or not we are in faith is simple because faith is always saying, doing or giving something.

When contemplating faith let's look no further than Abraham. He was a man who had his faults. Nevertheless, the Scripture reads he staggered not at the promise of God through unbelief, but he was strong in faith (Ro. 4:20).

At first glance, you can think the Scripture had a misprint when it read Abraham staggered not at the promise of God. However, through a closer examination we discover the Scripture to be accurate. All through Abraham's life we find him stumbling and staggering.

Yet when it counted the most Abraham kept his faith in God. God instructed Abraham to sacrifice his son Isaac. First, Abraham spoke by faith. Unsure of the outcome he told his servant the child and I will return (Ge. 22:5). Second, Abraham did not only talk the talk; he walked the walk. By faith he did something. Abraham and his young son climbed the mountain designated by God and made preparations to follow through with God's command (Ge. 22:9). Finally, Abraham by faith gave something. Abraham gave the gift of his son. And his gift moved both the heart and hand of God (Ge. 22:11-13).

Having faith in God dispels fear and releases the hold that fear can have on us. Therefore, we examine ourselves in accordance to the faith test. When we talk, act and give by faith we remove the limits from God and allow Him to do great and wonderful things. God desires to do things for us, but even more importantly; He desires to do things through us. Therefore, let's overcome fear by faith.

Chapter Two
Overcoming the Fear of Death

> But we had the sentence of death in ourselves, that we should not trust in ourselves, but in God which raiseth the dead: **Who delivered us from so great a death, and doth deliver**: in whom we trust that he will yet deliver us.
>
> —2nd Corinthians 1:9-10

The greatest fear a person will ever have to face is death. The fear of death like a boa constrictor creates a chokehold and attempts to strangle the life out of its victims. Jesus came so that we would experience life and watch it unfold with His grace and love. However, many people are unable to live a fulfilling life because they fear death. Their fear of death hinders them from exploring many of life's wonders or venturing beyond their daily routine.

Death: the Sum of All Fears

I am persuaded and convinced of the following idea. The sum of all fears is death and getting beyond the fear of death is the beginning of a life with less stress, struggle and strain. We can overcome stress by having faith in God because our faith cancels all fear, especially the fear of death. When we are unaffected by stress, any struggle and/or strain is removed.

Subsequently, the stress we encounter comes to test our resolve in Jesus, and it is equivalent to a crisis. No matter how we slice it, a crisis will do one of two things. It will help us *learn* more about the God of our faith or cause us to *lose* the faith we've placed in God.

The fear of death takes on many shapes. David pronounced he could walk through the valley of the shadow of death and fear no evil (Ps. 23:4). The shadow of death could be the condition of indebtedness, divorce or disease just to name a few. The fear of death is the fear of the unknown — the shadow.

People who are afraid of flying in an airplane are really afraid of dying in an airplane. Talking with these people will help us discover they're not fearful about the plane being in the air. They are horrified at the possibility of a crash.

David said, "I sought the Lord, and he heard me, and delivered me from all my fears. (Ps. 34:4)" David mentioned fear in the plural because there are many fears. Satan operates through fears. Therefore, we must conquer our fears in order to keep him from controlling our lives. The first book of the Bible depicts Satan as a serpent. However, by the time we get to the final book of the Bible he is described as a dragon. This is to say, if we do not gain control over the adversary he will grow to gain control over us.

The old fable Jack and the Beanstalk gave an account of a young boy who had to face a giant. Whenever the giant walked he would cry out, "Fee, Fi, Fo, Fum…" In like manner, the devil is as a roaring lion (or giant). However, the devil bellows, "FOD, FOP, FOR, FOF." These are the various kinds of fears in which the devil attacks us.

- FOD—Fear of Death
- FOP—Fear of People
- FOR—Fear of Rejection
- FOF—Fear of Failure

Death is the sum of all these fears. In other words, like a piece of thread woven through fabric, the fear of death is knitted into the fear of people, rejection and failure. Without the fear of death these other fears would lose their strength.

Facing the Fear of Death

David had to face, trace and erase his fears. He did not stand still in the valley of the shadow of death rather he walked through it. He was not paralyzed with doubt but rather energized through faith in God. David learned God can still hear us in our valleys even through his crisis.

We too must walk through our personal valley of the shadow of death and be willing to face, trace and erase our fears. After we erase our fears we must replace them with our faith in the living God.

The children of Israel faced the possibility of death at the hands of the Syrian army. The Scripture records Israel stood as two flocks of sheep while their enemy covered the country side. The Syrians were told that Israel's God had given them power in the hills but not in the valleys (1st Ki. 20:28). That day the Syrians learned a valuable lesson about God. God has power in the valleys as well as the hills of life. The Syrian army experienced defeat and Israel was delivered. The God who delivered Israel then will deliver us now if we are willing to face the fear of death.

The question becomes, "What is your fear?" Job said the thing he greatly feared came to him (Job 3:25). When it comes to fear, we may run but we can't hide. Therefore, it will do us good to find our fears before they find us. Confronting the fear of death destroys the power death can possess. Job feared losing his property, prosperity, and his posterity; and it happened. However, the Lord caused Job to remove his focus from the fear of death and concentrate on the God who created life.

I'm convinced that getting beyond the fear of death dispels other fears. The devil who roars, "FOD, FOP, FOR and FOF," won't be able to intimidate us. We will not live the life of God with the fear of death residing within us.

It's time to fight fire with fire! One of the ways firefighters fight fire or at least tame fire is with fire. Think about it. In order for a fire to spread it needs oxygen and fuel, which is found in vegetation. If the surrounding vegetation is burned, much of the oxygen and fuel is removed from the equation thus, the fire is controlled. In other words, when it comes to Satan we must meet aggression with aggression.

Terrorist groups aspiring martyrdom are only defeated by others who do not fear death. Overcoming the fear of death allows us to live without limits. We can have a supernatural, unusual and unbelievable lifestyle when the devil cannot intimidate us with death. Consequently, God causes the faithful not fearful to do mighty exploits.

Consider this account of Peter. He did the unimaginable. He boldly went where his friends and family dare not. Peter walked on water! At that moment in his life he was living without limits. Unfortunately the experience was short lived. Peter went from doing the unconceivable to not believing what he was doing. His incredible walk almost became a tragic wake. How could his fortune be turned to a misfortune so quickly? He became overwhelmed with the fear of death.

Can you imagine doing the mind-boggling? Think about the business God told you to start. How about reconciling ruined relationships? Where are the dreams you once kept near your heart? Why haven't you started? You think them impossible? With God all things are possible to them that believe. Face the fear of death and with God see your desires come alive.

From Death to Life

I am persuaded the child of God will never see death. Our physical bodies die daily, but our spiritual man is renewed day by day.

> Since these children are people with physical bodies, Jesus himself became like them. He did this so that, by dying, he could destroy the one who has the power of death—the devil—and free those who were like slaves all their lives **because of their fear of death**.
>
> —Hebrews 2:14-15 ncv

Jesus defeated Satan who had the power of death. The power of death is the fear of death. When you no longer fear dying, death loses its power. Now the children of God are positioned to move from death to life.

Mike Tyson was one of the most fearsome fighters to ever put on a pair of boxing gloves. His nickname was *Iron Mike* because of his brute strength.

Tyson is a former undisputed heavyweight champion of the world and holds the record as the youngest boxer to win the WBC, WBA and IBF heavyweight titles at 20 years, 4 months and 22 days old. Tyson won his first 19 professional bouts by knockout, with 12 of them occurring in the first round.

Many feared Tyson because of his ability, agility and his frightening reputation for punishing his opponents. One night the unthinkable occurred. The world of boxing and its fans were left stunned when 42-to-1 underdog James "Buster"

Douglas knocked Tyson out in round 10 causing him to lose his titles on February 11, 1990, in Tokyo, Japan.

The knockout victory by Douglas over Tyson has been described as one of the most shocking upsets in modern sports history.

Mike Tyson who was considered by most to be a menace in the ring was shamefully defeated by a virtually unknown. How was Douglas able to defeat Mike Tyson and shock the world? Well, placing preparation, skill, and reach/height advantage aside, Douglas was at an emotional peak after losing his mother to a stroke 23 days prior to the fight. He fought the fight of his life. I believe somehow this brush with death served as a catalyst for Douglas to ultimately stand victorious.

Likewise, Jesus' brush with death makes it possible to remove the fear of death so we too can stand victorious in life. He defeated the devil and took away the power of the fear of death. Jesus destroyed death when He rose the third day after His crucifixion. Jesus holds the keys to death and hell (Re. 1:18) and through Him we are more than conquerors.

According to the book of Hebrews, every man must die once (Heb. 9:27). Therefore, every man must determine if they will die to themselves and live for Jesus; or live for themselves and one day experience eternal death. This decision is critical and essential to our Christian walk. When we receive Jesus and allow Him to be Lord over our lives, we pass from death to life.

This death is not a physical death it is a spiritual matter. However, when we die to ourselves and live for Jesus we no longer need to fear a physical death. Without Jesus, the physical death is painful. Nevertheless, with Jesus the physical death is pain-free. Those who live without Christ can only look forward to torment. Those who live for Christ have eternal life to discover and enjoy.

A couple was on an airplane. Without warning, the pilot instructed the passengers to brace themselves for severe turbulence. As the plane shook violently the wife began crying; but the husband shouted, "Hallelujah! This is what we've been talking about and praying for, we're going to see Jesus!" The wife struck her husband and shouted, "I want to see Jesus; just not right now!"

Once you understand the concept of passing from death to life you can handle fear. You'll understand fear is an act of your will, not merely an emotion of what you feel. You can choose to be faithful in fearful circumstances. My spiritual father says, "You may tremble on the Rock—many people do; but the Rock will never tremble under you."

The child of God need not tremble nor be in terror when it comes to the subject of death. We are no longer subjugated to death because death has no power, more importantly death has no pain.

Chapter Three

Is There Pain in Death?

> …But is now made manifest by the appearing of our Savior Jesus Christ, **who hath abolished death, and hath brought life** and immortality to light through the gospel.
>
> —2nd Timothy 1:10

Yes, there is pain in death for those who are without God. Regret, sorrow and fear are a few emotions that can plague people when death comes. However, the pain that accompanies death is not only emotional; it can be mental and physical.

On the other hand, the born-again believer can look forward to death. Of course I love my family, friends and the many relationships I've developed throughout the years and I have a desire to remain here to enjoy them. By the same token, I desire to come face to face with my Lord and Redeemer—Jesus.

I don't fear death and neither should you. The reason we need not fear death is because there is no pain in death to the Believer.

Death Has No Sting

> The last enemy that shall be destroyed is death. **O death, where is thy sting?** O grave, where is thy victory?
>
> —1st Corinthians 15: 26, 55

The Believer can shout right now, "O death, where is thy sting?" The sting of death is the fear of death. Listen, when a child of God dies, they do not see death. Therefore, we have no reason to fear it. For this purpose, death has lost its' sting. The child of God moves from a position of death to a place of life in Jesus Christ (Eph. 2:5).

According to the Bible, I believe when a child of God dies, they wake up and see Jesus (2nd Cor. 5:8). It's a transition we make, from one life into the next. There is no intermittent time. There is no pause. There is no purgatory. It's either heaven or hell. Before we know it we're standing in the presence of the Lord.

A mother sat watching as her son and daughter played in the park. Without warning her son began screaming. The mother detected something was wrong. She immediately investigated the scene.

She discovered her son had been stung by a bee. Soon after, her daughter became frightened. The mother asked the girl why was she afraid. The girl exclaimed, "I do not want the bee to sting me."

The mother pulled the bee's stinger out of her son's skin and showed it to her daughter. Reassuring the girl of her safety, the mother said, "The bee can no longer hurt anyone because he has lost his stinger and ultimately his life." Like that bee, death has lost its stinger and the devil has lost his power over us.

Allow me to say, there is pain in the dying process, but

not in death itself. When Jesus was crucified He destroyed the devil's power. It must be understood: **Jesus has taken the sting out of death!**

Many of us are waiting to pass from life to death; but Jesus said we have passed from death unto life (Joh. 5:24). This gives us hope. When circumstances look bleak we know death is not the final outcome, life always prevails. We will not come to death!

I get excited when thinking about Jesus' gift. He's granted us life. Even more astounding, He's removed the pain of death.

I stated earlier, there is pain in the dying process, but not in the death experience. Allow me to explain this further. To say there is pain in the dying process, but not in the death experience may sound like a play on semantics. However, this concept is much more than semantics. It goes beyond reason into the realm of revelation.

As long as we are in our earthly bodies we'll undergo aches and pains. We will experience toothaches, backaches and a whole lot of heartaches. Our "growing pains," are indicative of the dying process. However, after the earthly death the child of God is given a new body. These new bodies won't experience bunions, bulges or bi-focals; they won't drag, sag or lag. Our new bodies will be given unlimited ability, agility and stability.

We're going through the death process now, and there is pain in it; but when we come to death itself, there is no pain for the child of God. God raised Jesus from the dead and set him free from the pain of death (Acts 2:24). His freedom became our freedom also.

When my dentist pulled my tooth I felt absolutely no pain (neither did I feel my lip or mouth for that matter). The reason is because he gave me Novocain. This anesthetic caused the nerves in my mouth to become numb. The dental experience was real, but I didn't feel any of it. In like manner, the death experience is real, but we won't feel it.

Beloved, death has no sting nor does it have any pain.

Death Has Lost its Prisoners

> Forasmuch then as the children are partakers of flesh and blood, he also himself likewise took part of the same; that through death he might destroy him that had the power of death, that is, the devil; And deliver them who through fear of death were all their lifetime *subject to bondage*.
>
> —Hebrews 2:14-15

What is your attitude concerning the subject of death? I ask this question because your answer determines whether you're a prisoner to death or not. Those who see death as a dark presence lurking just beyond every corner will stay in a place of fear. These are superstitious people. They have conniptions if they break a mirror, walk under a ladder or exercise any of the superstitions that stem from the fear of death.

A wealthy man visited a zoo. He spent the day admiring various animals. Finally, he saw an enormous elephant. The elephant was chained to a pole which restricted his movement. The entire day, every day, the elephant could only take three steps forward and three steps backward.

This man pitied the elephant and felt the restriction was harsh. He purchased the elephant and shipped it back to its natural environment. The man figured the elephant would be free to roam in the wild. However, once there minus the chains, the elephant continued to walk three steps forward and three steps backward. The elephant had been conditioned to a life of restriction.

Many of God's people are much like that elephant.

Even though Jesus removed the pain of death, they remain prisoners to the fear of death and are thereby restricted.

None of us have to remain a prisoner to death or a slave to the devil. How can we experience true liberation? Jesus said when we know the truth we are made free (Joh. 8:32). The truth is death has no pain! The Believer has a greater life to gain and death is just a door to that life.

Consider God's servants Paul and Silas. They were beaten, wrongfully imprisoned and placed in the depths of jail, chained to thick wooden blocks. The situation was desperate. The two men waited to hear the judgment of the Roman rulers.

These men could have complained and they certainly had every reason to do so. However, rather than having a pity party they chose to throw God a praise party. They had the right attitude and lifted their voices not with dry rehearsed renditions. They offered up symphonies of spontaneity. These men didn't soak and sour about their suffering. They praised the Lord because He was present in their suffering.

As a result, the earth shook in such a way the chains were broken and the prison doors were opened. Something miraculous happens when we praise God. If we learn to face death with a shout instead of doubt, our praise will loose us from every form of bondage.

The Lord doesn't want His people settling for bondage living which is a life of limitations. This kind of life keeps us from experiencing God's very best.

Remember, the children of Israel were subject to bondage for 400 years by the hands of the Egyptians. Through fear and intimidation one generation after the next was forced into labor. Many nights were spent crying to God for relief and release.

God sent His servant Moses to demand the discharge

of His people. The Egyptian Pharaoh responded with a proposition. He told Moses, "I'll allow you to sacrifice to the LORD your God in the wilderness, only don't go very far." Consequently, God had more in mind. He was taking Israel out of Egypt.

Accordingly, He desires to do the same for His people today. To walk with God is to live a life without limitations, a life where all things become possible. However, the devil much like the Pharaoh wants to keep us in bondage. We must not allow ourselves to be imprisoned, but rather keep the right perception.

The Apostle Paul possessed the right attitude concerning death and bondage. He declared, "For me to live is Christ, and to die is gain." Paul further admitted having a desire to *depart* and be with Christ (Phil. 1:21-23). It's interesting to note how Paul spoke of dying. He used the word depart because he understood death is not annihilation; it is separation. Annihilation denotes ceasing to exist. Separation connotes relocating. Anyone would fear annihilation which is bondage, while separation conveys death as a transition which means to depart.

I fly on planes often and I have yet to see anyone dreading their flight's departure. Now, there are times when we do not want to leave loved ones. Even then, separating is understood as relocation not dislocation. Do you want to live free from bondage? Begin by viewing death as a separation not annihilation.

Rest in Peace

Usually when we hear the term rest in peace we think of dying. However, to rest in peace one need not experience physical death. We can rest in peace while living because the abundant life of Jesus starts with having His peace.

We cannot have the peace of God until we have peace

with God. Receiving Jesus Christ as the Lord over our lives gives us peace with Him. Once we have peace with God we have what is called His eternal life.

Eternal life is not to be confused with everlasting life. Eternal life is the *zoe*, or nature of God's life. Everlasting life is what we experience when passing from this existence to the next. In other words, we live forever!

While we still have breath, God wants us to live a life without fear. The Lord expects us to replace fear with His peace. One primary way to accomplish this is by understanding death. To the born again Believer, death is like sleeping.

> But I would not have you to be ignorant, brethren, concerning them which are *asleep*, that ye sorrow not, even as others which have no hope. For if we believe that Jesus died and rose again, even so them which *sleep* in Jesus will God bring with him.
> —1st Thessalonians 4:13-14

The aforementioned scripture describes the dead in Christ as just sleeping. Having this understanding allows us to rest in peace.

The Bible records several accounts where danger and even death was eminent, but those who faced the danger simply went to sleep.

— Daniel was faithful to God. For that reason, he was placed in the lions' den. By all accounts, Daniel was lions' lunch. He was to be a human hotdog. Daniel was dinner and these ferocious felines were hungry.

A predicament like this calls for pacing. Under normal circumstances panic would be just what the doctor ordered. Who would blame Daniel if he begged his captors for mercy? Oddly enough, he did not beg; he chose to go to bed.

Daniel knew the power of his God. Therefore, he did not fear death. He took the first catnap!

— Peter was arrested. Some of his fellow disciples had already been assassinated. He had been incarcerated before, but this time he sat on death row. Word of his execution was highly publicized. His security detail had been beefed up in order to prohibit his escape.

The next day would be his last day. Surely Peter should have been frantic. After all, the believers were up all night praying on his behalf. Rather than meditate on his demise he chose to doze.

— Jesus was in the stern of the ship. His disciples were atop the boat baffled and belligerent. Every crash of the waves tested the boat's integrity. The angry winds challenged the progression of their sail. The force of the rain hammered down like nails.

The disciples decided to seek the aid of the Savior. Much to their dismay they found Him not struggling or strategizing—He was slumbering. While the disciples were catching waves; Jesus was catching winks. Jesus did not fall asleep; He went to sleep. We know this because the Scripture says He had a pillow. His sleeping was not delinquent it was deliberate.

They woke Him with aggression and accusations. They challenged His sensitivity; He changed the scene to serenity. Then He posed a question for the storms of all ages. Jesus said, "Why are you so fearful?"

Fear disturbs our rest. Daniel, Peter and Jesus displayed the same response when faced with death. When it was easy to panic they chose to rest in peace.

Think about these prototypes, Enoch and Elijah. They were taken by God without having to experience a physical death. I believe God through the Scripture is using their accounts to make a spiritual point. Like these men, our physical death will be a translation.

Enoch would not see death because he pleased God (Heb. 11:5). Elijah took a limo ride to heaven (2 Ki. 2:11). When our faith pleases God we can rest in peace.

When Jesus was informed of His good friend Lazarus' death He looked to comfort His disciples by acknowledging that Lazarus was asleep. Jesus compared Lazarus' physical death to slumber (Joh. 11:11). On another account a young girl lay dead. Again, Jesus referred to her as only sleeping (Mk. 5:39).

There is no need to fear death because Jesus has removed the pain of death. And to the restless Jesus offers, "I leave you peace; my peace I give you…So don't let your hearts be troubled or afraid."

Chapter Four
Overcoming the Fear of People

> Then I said unto you, Dread not, **neither be afraid of them**.
> —Deuteronomy 1:29

Throughout the years I have counseled people concerning their fears. Of all the fears and believe me there were many, the one most salient is the fear of people.

It's absolutely amazing how some people allow other people to hinder their progress in life. God longs to see us grow and fulfill our purpose; therefore it is imperative we overcome the fear of people.

Living the God inspired life requires us not to be intimidated by others. Whenever we submit to the fear of people our faith in God is decreased. Frankly, we should not fear people's sum, size or strength. The fear of people is eliminated when we see beyond them and focus on God.

Seeing Beyond the Sum of People

The Believers confidence should not rest on the strength of men, but on the strength of God. By the same token, we should not allow the number of men to intimidate us from pursuing Him. Sometimes it appears that obeying God places us in the minority. However, standing with God is always the place of majority. He is greater than all those who stand oppose to His will for us. Therefore, we must be confident in His sovereignty.

Consider the following scripture:

> "…for he hath said, I will never leave thee, nor forsake thee. So that we may boldly say, The Lord is my helper, and **I will not fear what man shall do unto me**."
>
> —Hebrews 13:5-6 kjv (emphasis added)

The writer of this passage understood three very important things. First, God will never leave us. Second, the Lord is our helper. Finally, we need not fear whatever men devise against us.

The Bible tells of a woman who was stricken with pain. In the span of twelve years this woman suffered with severe hemorrhaging. Because of this issue she was isolated from family and friends; as a recluse, she craved relief.

Her money was squandered on medical treatment that never produced the cure; her hopes of recovery tattered from one broken promise to the next. She was disconnected and rejected by the community at large.

One day she received word of a man who worked wonders, a healer who helped. Someone told her about Jesus and His power to deliver the bruised, battered, and broken. Then she yearned the day for a chance encounter with this Miracle Man whose knack was changing negatives into positives.

Unannounced, Jesus came in close proximity of this woman. Her thoughts began leaping around in her head. "Can He heal me? Will He heal me?" Finally she decided to approach Him. However, there was one major problem. A great crowd of people stood between this woman's hurt and the Healer.

Jesus was surrounded by a mob that grew larger by the minute. By law this woman's physical condition disallowed her public appearance. In fact, to be seen in public should have meant death. Although this woman faced a great dilemma, she pressed through the hostile crowd.

Her help was within arm's reach; her deliverance within earshot. The only thing that stood between her and Jesus was the crazed crowd. She was forced to choose between playing it safe or risking it all.

Fortunately, she saw beyond the sum of the people and focused her faith on the Son of God. She exchanged her issue for Jesus' virtue. Because she dared touch God He in turn touched her.

No account in the Bible depicts getting over the fear of the sum of people more than Gideon's.

For years Israel had been exploited by the Midianites, a bunch of roughnecks whose mode of operation was to pilfer the surrounding territories. They were hotshot hooligans who liked to flex their muscle on the weak. Therefore, they took their leisure at the expense of Israel's loses.

Growing weary of the whippings, Israel decided to head for the hills. They had lost more than their share of livestock and land at the hands of these Mediterranean Mad Men. And if matters couldn't get worse, the Midianites united with another outlaw bunch called the Amalekites. And together, they forced Israel into penury and submission.

Finally, enough was enough! Israel cried and asked God to deliver them from the might of their foes. God responded. However, His solution seemed less than suitable. When Israel was outnumbered God called for the odd man out—Gideon.

Born into the smallest tribe of the nation of Israel, Gideon felt less than ready for the task at hand. God was ready to kick tail; Gideon was thinking tuck tail. God came to defend Israel's name, and He wanted to use a no-name to do it.

However, the only confidence Gideon possessed was in the amount of soldiers he retained. Gideon was counting heads while God was checking hearts. In one day God reduced Gideon's military might to a small group of men. God wanted Israel's total dependency upon Him.

The day of battle had arrived. Israel's enemy encompassed them about. They covered the plain like a swarm of locusts and appeared as grains of sand on the seashore. Perhaps Gideon sensed intuitively the sum of the enemy was not greater than the size of his God.

Moving beyond fear he commanded his few hundred against tens of thousands. What happened next was nothing less than a miracle. God's reign brought the enemy's ruin.

Ponder the following passage:

I will not be afraid of ten thousands of people,
that have set themselves against me round
about.
—Psalm 3:6 kjv

Beloved, there is no need to fear the sum of people when we stand with the God of the universe. Once beyond the sum, we must understand that size doesn't matter.

Seeing Beyond the Size of People

Question! How do you receive God's ability? Well, the answer is right under your nose. You receive God's ability to accomplish anything through the Word He releases.

Every word God speaks carries with it the promise of victory. When God speaks to us He looks to empower us and move us toward our destiny. The Word of God changes everything. It turns negatives to positives and brings light out of darkness.

The devil will intimidate us if we allow him. He's the proverbial bully on the playground. Bullies seek the weak. They use their size to intimidate, manipulate and dominate.

Have you ever stood in the sun and cast a shadow on the wall? Depending on your position relative to the sun, your shadow could be larger than your physical body. This is the case with the devil. He looks to position himself where he is able to cast a tall shadow, but he's actually smaller than he appears.

The devil knows God's Word gives us strength. He attempts to speak over the Word of God with the voices of fear. He says things like, "You're not loved." "What's the use? You'll never have enough." In essence, the devil tries to use big problems or big people to make us feel small.

Goliath was a mammoth of a man. As the champion of the Philistines he hurled accusations and spewed challenges. As a solid soldier of fortune, Goliath paralyzed the entire army of Israel with his size.

Goliath stretched over 9 feet tall. The armor he sported was the weight of three heavy men. His sword made of iron could cut through trees like butter. This instrument of Satan was itching for hand-to-hand combat.

At a time when everyone feared, a young David had faith. David saw beyond Goliath's size to see his prize. The king of Israel promised many rewards to the man who could defeat this giant.

David had the inside track to this latest challenge. He had what all the others didn't. He had confidence that the Lord would deliver. David's faith in God's mission superseded Goliath's mass. David didn't see Goliath's frame as too big to match; he saw him as too big to miss.

Empowered by God, David defeated Goliath, received his rewards and eventually occupied the throne. When we take God at His word we are equipped and energized to defeat the devil every time.

When we are weak, God's Word says we're strong. When we are surrounded by poverty, God's Word enables us to become rich. All we need is God's Word and like David we can topple the giants that stand against us.

God's Word allows us to live life without fear. Once we overcome the fear of people's sum and size all that's left is to overcome their strength.

Seeing Beyond the Strength of People

In the Old Testament God led Israel by a cloud. This cloud was a physical representation of His presence. However, many were lost because they didn't follow the cloud; they followed the influence of the crowd. Rather than trusting in God's presence they relied on powerful people. They missed God's assurance due to other's influence.

Instead of relying upon the will of God for Israel, Aaron allowed the influence of powerful men to move him to build an idol in the wilderness. Saul sacrificed strange offerings because he feared people's rejection. Korah and his company manipulated people to go against God's will and many lives were lost. These are just a few examples of what can occur when we are influenced by the strength of others.

This is certainly the case today. Many of God's children have accepted the limitations placed on them by others. Some may say we can't; God says we can. Others may say we aren't; God says we are.

On most airlines there are class restrictions based upon the arrangement of seats. There is first class, business class and coach (often considered no class). However, I have determined in my heart no matter where I'm seated I'm first class and so are you because we're children of the Most High God. Above all, we're seated in heavenly places with Christ Jesus, and there is no higher class than that.

God has allowed me to pastor thousands and employ hundreds and I'm humbled over this fact.

One day the foreman of one of our building projects approached me. He expressed his amazement over the size of our church. He further conveyed how he was particularly impressed with my leadership. Interested by his comments, I asked him to explain further.

He said if he led our sized church and staff he would use his power to dominate rather than develop the people. I was quite surprised by his confession and immediately explained the heart of a godly leader. This man was walking proof that absolute power can corrupt absolutely.

Sadly, there are many who use their authority to intimidate others. For that reason, we must know the power of God so we never fear the strength of men. Jesus speaking to His disciples admonished them not to fear men who can only kill the body, but to fear God who has the power to kill both soul and body (Matt. 10:28).

The king of Babylon set up a massive golden statue. Then he released an edict stating whenever his music was played everyone had to bow down and worship the image.

This proclamation was to be obeyed throughout the province. Those who would not comply would be placed in a furnace of fire. There were three men of God positioned to handle the Babylonian king's affairs. They were aware of the decree; however, they were not in agreement with it.

One day the music was playing and all but these three bowed and worshipped the statue. Malicious men reported their insurrection to the king, and because of his own law, he was forced to punish them. The king asked Shadrach, Meshach, and Abednego to explain their defiance.

These men of God offered the king the creed of life for every Believer. They boldly confessed, "Our God is able to deliver us—He will deliver us—but even if He chooses not to deliver us—be it known, we will not serve your gods nor worship your golden image."

These men of God were fully aware of the king's authority. They knew one word from the king could end their lives. Emotions were hot and tempers tested. Rather than fearing the strength of men, they rested in the sovereignty of God. The king demanded their alliance and quickly saw God had their allegiance.

Sure enough they were thrown in the fiery furnace. However their loyalty was rewarded with God's security. The king was introduced to the Master's mathematics. He asked, "Did not we throw *three* men in the furnace? I see *four* men loose and walking in the fire without harm."

They were bound and cast into the furnace of fire. However, their chains were loosed in Christ's presence. We are never alone in our fires. We will always have God's protection and His presence when faced with pressure. When Jesus rules our lives the world's restrictions are released. We don't have to fear the strength of men because our God is stronger.

My friend, a life without limitations is possible once we see beyond the sum, size and strength of people. In every situation we must factor God into the equation. See Him as He is; large and in charge. We may not know what the future holds, but we know Who holds the future—God.

God is not just the Alpha He is the Omega. He is not just the Beginning He is the End. We can't see Him as the Author without knowing Him as the Finisher. In essence, don't consider some of God; acknowledge all of God.

The same God who keeps the orbits aligned in His hand keeps us in His heart; and we do not have to fear people.

Chapter Five
Overcoming the Fear of Rejection

> If the world hate you, ye know that it hated me before it hated you. If ye were of the world, the world would love his own: but because ye are not of the world, but **I have chosen you out of the world, therefore the world hateth you**.
>
> —John 15:18-19

Rejection can be a hard pill to swallow. Consider the child who is forced to grow up without the love of a parent; the spouse who is refused emotional support; or the termination notice given after years of faithful service on the job. These are just a few examples of rejection and in all cases the rejected person may feel inadequate or insignificant.

No one likes to be rejected. However, rejection is very much a part of life. No matter who you are or where you are, somehow rejection has a way of surfacing. To be a child of God we must expect rejection. I will even go as far as to say we must embrace it.

In order to progress with God we must have the ability to face and not fear rejection. Have you ever heard the saying,

"You can't please all the people all the time?" Well, let me add, some people can't be pleased anytime. In others words, not everyone will like you or me, but that's okay. It's up to us to remain pleasant as much as possible, but we don't have to please everyone.

Jesus noted the world hates. He said the world hated Him and will therefore hate those who follow Him. Jesus' use of the word "hate" in this context describes a person who is in the dark and rejects the light. In essence, there will be those who will detest us because of the light of God within us.

I made it up in my mind long ago, I will not be ashamed of the light; rather I will share the light. It's a sad commentary when Believers fail to allow the light of Christ to shine for fear of rejection. Even worse, many go along to get along. That is to say, they bend and pretend because they desire the acceptance of others.

Rejection is a two-sided coin. On one side, we must embrace rejection while on the other side; we must be capable of rejecting anything that is opposed to the will of God.

Therefore, make the decision now to be a God-pleaser rather than a man-pleaser.

MEN-PLEASERS ARE DELUDED

Going through life attempting to gain the acceptance of everyone will prove tiresome. Above that, you'll discover it is impossible.

Those who think it's possible to please everyone are deceived. Furthermore, it is impossible to follow God and please the crowd at the same time. Great men have discovered this very fact.

Ponder the following scripture written by the Apostle Paul:

> Do you think I am trying to make people accept me? No, God is the One I am trying to please. Am I trying to please people? If I still wanted to please people, I would not be a servant of Christ.
>
> –Galatians 1:10 ncv

At one point Paul was striving to please people; and that caused him to persecute the Church of God.

Interestingly, Paul was a Jew evident by his name "Saul" which happened to be the name of Israel's first king. Coincidently, both men were from the tribe of Benjamin. On the other hand, his name "Paul" was a Roman name signifying his Roman citizenship.

Paul referred to himself as "a Hebrew of Hebrews" (Phil. 3:5) because he held his Jewish heritage in high regards. He was raised in Jerusalem by his own admission "at the feet of Gamaliel" a revered rabbi of his day (Acts 5:34).

All of this pointed to the fact that Paul walked lock step to the Jewish law. He cared what others thought of him and labored to be accepted and respected within the hierarchy of the Jewish community. He and his contemporaries ensured that the law and its traditions were followed to the letter.

Above everything else, Paul truly believed he was a crusader for God sent to rid the population of the heretics called "Christians." In his zeal to protect the law of God and comply with the will of men, Paul persecuted the church of God beyond measure. He believed he was punishing those guilty of offending God. What he believed to be fair was fault, his acts of deliverance were actually deluded.

While Paul rode his high horse to Damascus, Jesus revealed Himself. He told Paul He was alive and greater than the Jewish law. Paul was convicted, convinced and ultimately converted. Then he began defending the same Jesus he had defamed.

Paul was knocked off his high horse trying to please men then; and if we're not careful, it will yield the same experience for us now. Paul used the law as an excuse to please men. What excuses are we using today?

Paul discovered pleasing men pulls us away from serving God. Jesus said those who find life shall lose it, but those who lose their life for my sake shall find it (Matt. 16:25). Through serving God we learn to trust His sovereignty. Men will lead us astray, but God knows the exact path to get us to our destiny.

When we fear being rejected by men we'll bend over backwards hoping to fit in. The problem with fitting in with men is copying and coveting. In the end, we become counterfeits not originals. The fear of rejection invites us to fake it until we make it. However, when we fake it we'll never make it.

No matter how we see it, trying to please men is a deception because our happiness is not found in men it dwells with God.

God-pleasers are Delighted

To gain fulfillment and delight we must aim to please God. The truth is when God is happy we are happy. Trying to receive happiness without considering God is dangerous. The Scripture tells us the Lord is the judge of men and He will repay wrong acts. The writer of the book of Hebrews warns it's a terrible thing to fall into the hands of a living God (Heb. 10:30-31).

Think about it. The Lord is alive! Therefore, to live life without desiring to please Him is evil. If we spell the word live backwards it spells evil. In essence, leaving God out of our lives is backward living and it's evil.

One afternoon a father told his son to turn the volume on the television down. In protest the boy complained he wanted the TV to remain loud. The father approached his son and gave this reprimand: "Son, if I'm happy, you've got a good chance of being happy."

He further explained, "Your being upset changes nothing. However, if I get upset I can change your whole environment." It's the same way with God. If we get upset our situation may not change. Nevertheless, if our attitude gets the Lord upset there can be radical repercussions. Make no mistake; it behooves us to please God.

Samuel sat pondering the demands of Israel. He could not quite grasp the request placed on him by the people. They wanted a king to rule over their affairs and to fight their battles. Samuel knew they already had the King of kings.

He felt betrayed and betwixt. After all his years of service how could the people reject him? Where did they get off asking for a king when they were under the covering of the Master of the universe? While Samuel sizzled in indignation God spoke to him:

> Listen to whatever the people say to you. They have not rejected you. They have rejected me from being their king. They are doing as they have always done...
> —1st Samuel 8:7-8

God was ensuring Samuel the people's rejection was not directed at him, but at God Himself. He also wanted Samuel to know He (God) could take rejection. This is indicated by the statement "They are doing as they have always done." The Lord taught Samuel rejection was a part of life.

Although Samuel felt rejected by the people he found delight knowing he was accepted by God. God's delight in Samuel's service propelled him through his suffering.

When we delight ourselves in the Lord He gives us

the desires of our heart (Ps. 37:4). Delighting ourselves in the Lord means we are focused on Him and what He wants for us. God knows us better than we know ourselves and He is fully aware of what it takes to please us. When we please Him, He in turn pleases us.

You Have Been Accepted

I challenge you to think about those times when you have been accepted. Discovering you made the team; initiated into the club; receiving a favorable response to your proposal were all moments of exhilaration because you were accepted.

We all have had those moments. In fact we live for them and almost to a fault. If not cognizant, we can fall victim to the fear of rejection all while going after the feeling of acceptance.

The simple fact is this, we are already accepted! God who created us with a purpose in mind has accepted us within His heart. We are uniquely and wonderfully made and if we do not understand this we'll have an identity crisis which ultimately leads to identity theft.

People who are not comfortable in their skin or confused about who they are try to become someone else. The person who is searching for their identity may commit identity theft by taking on another's personality. When you fear the rejection of others this possibility can become a reality.

God doesn't want any of us feeling insignificant. He has hand crafted us and He embraces us as we desire to become more like Him.

A little boy hand crafted a wooden boat in which he engraved his initials. While playing with his boat at the lakeside on a rainy day, it was pulled by the current and drifted away.

The boy was saddened for weeks. One day while in town, the boy passed a pawnshop and noticed his boat in the window. He hastened into the store and informed the shop owner that the boat was his.

The shop owner asked how the boy knew this was his boat. The boy examined the boat and noticed it had been painted but his initials were still carved in the wood. The shop owner explained how he bought the boat from another kid just weeks earlier. He told the boy he could have the boat back if he was willing to pay for it.

Without hesitation the boy ensured the store owner of his intent to reclaim his boat. The boy performed odd jobs to earn money to purchase his prized possession. Days later the boy returned to the pawnshop with money in hand. He bought the boat and while exiting the store he said with excitement, "Little boat, I love you twice as much now because I made you, lost you, and now I've paid to get you back!"

Beloved, the Lord loves and accepts us. He made us and then He lost us; but glory be to God, He paid the price and redeemed us.

The Scripture conveys it pleased God to adopt us into His family and that we are accepted by Him (Eph. 1:5-6). I don't know about you, but this gives me a warm feeling all over. Just to think that God adopted us. It's one thing to be born into a family, but an adoption carries another connotation.

When someone is adopted that means they have been hand-picked by their parents. You can't be adopted by mistake. The process of adoption is critical and tedious. The parents are vetted by the adoption agency. The parents' privacy is invaded and the amazing thing is they welcome scrutiny all for the sake of gaining the child.

This is what God has done. He took on the form of man and allowed Himself to be scrutinized and worse, scourged in order to adopt us into His family. He didn't adopt us with blind-folds on. He saw who we were and out of the muck and mire He cleaned us and claimed us. We are adopted and even better—accepted.

Just knowing we are accepted should be enough to help us overcome the fear of rejection.

Chapter Six
Learning To Just Say No

Jesus said to them…**I cannot choose who will sit at my right or left**; those places belong to those for whom my Father has prepared them.

—Matthew 20:23 ncv

There is an old tale of a young brave who desired to earn his first feather. According to his tribal custom each feather represented a level of manhood and an act of bravery.

So the young brave decided to climb the highest mountain in his village. Upon reaching the top he was startled by a rattle snake. While contemplating his escape, much to his amazement, the snake spoke.

The snake asked the brave to carry him down the mountain. Albeit, the brave wisely denied the request fearing the snake would bite. However, the snake begged and promised the brave he would not. Feeling pressured, the brave conceded to the snakes petition.

After arriving at the bottom of the mountain and in the company of his tribe, the brave pulled the snake from his pouch and placed it on the ground. Without warning, the snake rose and bit him.

Totally stunned the brave cried, "You said you wouldn't bite me." While hissing the snake replied, "Yeah, but you knew what I was when you picked me up."

Many go through life getting snake bitten because they fear saying no. We must not fear being rejected or fear rejecting the unrighteous requests of others.

Some find saying no a difficult task. The reason is simple, they want to be accepted. Therefore, they go through life looking to please others at all costs. This is not the kind of life God desires for His children. Hearing the word "No" may hurt, but believe me it can also help.

Living without limits doesn't mean everything is good for us. It is simply not allowing fear to hold us back when God has released us to move forward. The fear of rejection is spawn out of a longing for acceptance. Therefore, God loves and accepts us in order to ignite the spirit of faith within us.

People who are incapable of accepting rejection can be dangerous. The first murder ever committed was as a result of the inability to accept rejection. Cain murdered his twin brother Abel. The Bible records God accepted Abel's gift, but did not accept Cain's.

God informed Cain if he did well his gift would be received. Overwhelmed by God's refusal Cain decided to attack his brother. This hideous act was perpetrated because Cain felt rejected by God. Understand when God rejects anything about us it's for our good.

Throughout the years I have heard people say concerning their prayers to God, "I'm waiting on an answer." Some of these people have been waiting on an answer for years. Allow me to insert this thought; the answer might be "No." I'm not opposed to waiting on the Lord. In fact, I teach patience is important to receive what we need. Oddly enough, some believe God's answer is always "Yes," but this is not true.

The only prayers God grants a yes to are His own. In other words, when we petition the Lord for something it must line up according to His Word. If our requests stem from selfish pursuits the answer will always be no. Keep in mind God's no is not to hurt, it's to help. For this reason, there are times when we need to say no, as well.

Saying No to Family

Family plays an important role in our lives. We count on family for love and support. I take my time with family seriously and relish the moments we share together. However, there are times when we need to say no to those we love.

Some parents can never say no to their children. These parents cater to their child's demands, and this kind of pampering is detrimental to the child's development. Some believe they are raising an Einstein when actually they are raising a Frankenstein. The point is not to spoil our family, but to grow together in the Kingdom of God.

Jesus had just begun His career in the ministry, and while teaching, He was abruptly interrupted. Someone told Him that His mother and siblings stood outside the church and desired to see Him.

Did Jesus stop teaching to go see what His family wanted? As a matter of fact He didn't. Instead, Jesus profoundly stated His mother, brother and sister were those who did the will of God (Matt. 12:46-50). In essence, Jesus said no to their request for a private meeting outside of God's agenda.

It's important to recognize God's will has to be placed above even our family. Jesus said He came to separate mother from daughter and father from son (Matt. 10:34-37). Jesus' statement is paramount because without it we can allow family to separate us from God.

Leah was Jacob's first wife, but she wasn't his first choice. As a matter of fact, she wasn't his choice at all. By some accounts she was not attractive on the outside; her beauty was carried within her heart. Like any other girl she dreamt of her wedding day. I'm sure she imagined her groom's gleam as he pronounced his undying love for her. I guess she envisioned a bright star-lit evening and brilliant decorations. She probably wanted a guest list fitting for a princess.

Consequently, none of that mattered. What she desired and what she received stood in stark contrast. Instead of a highly publicized ceremony she was given a private closed circuit session. Rather than showing off her stunning hair her face was covered with a hood. Before she was given Jacob's name she had to assume her younger sister Rachel's name. Her wedding was far from a parade it was a charade.

This sham of a wedding was a prelude to an anticlimactic marriage. Jacob gave his sincere attention and affections to his second wife Rachel while Leah had to receive scraps of time and touches. Then it happened! Leah became pregnant with Jacob's first child. The Scripture reveals the Lord saw Leah's rejection by Jacob (Gen. 29:31). For this reason, God opened Leah's womb. Surely she felt having this child would close the chasm in their relationship.

Their first son Reuben's name meant *friend or companion*. She said now surely my husband will love me (Gen. 29:32). However, it didn't happen. Leah conceived a second son whom she named Simeon which means *hearing*. She said surely the Lord has heard I was hated (Gen. 29:33). Then she conceived their third son Levi whose name means *a joining*. She thought surely this child will cause my husband and I to be joined together (Gen. 29:34). Again her hopes were dashed.

While swimming in the sea of rejection Leah learned to lean upon the Lord. She gave birth to their fourth son who she named Judah meaning *praise the Lord*. Leah discovered there was more peace in pleasing God than there was in trying to please her husband. She finally stood up and faced her husband's rejection. In essence, Leah finally said no more will I feel inadequate or allow my family to make me feel insignificant.

There was a man who was a real miser when it came to his money. He loved money more than anything or anyone, and just before he died he made a demand of his wife: "When I die, place all my money in my casket, so I can take it to the afterlife."

His wife promised him she would fulfill his request. One day he died. At the funeral he lay stretched in the casket and the wife sat in the front row dressed in black. At the conclusion of the ceremony the wife placed a small box in his casket.

The wife's sister asked, "I know you weren't foolish enough to place all that man's money in the casket with him, were you?" The wife responded, "I promised I would, so I wrote him a check."

A major part of overcoming the fear of rejection is the ability to say no to family. Saying no becomes imperative when we sense their selfish pursuits. A "No" is not always expressed with our words, sometimes it is displayed by our actions.

SAYING NO TO FRIENDS

Friends are great to have in life. They can be supportive and encouraging. However, there are times when friends are wrong and we must let them know it. It's no easy task to reprove a friend. Likewise, it's not easy to say no to a friend, but sometimes saying no is just what's needed.

King Solomon had a son by the name of Rehoboam

who when Solomon died took command of the throne. Rehoboam called for all the people to be gathered in order to hear their hearts. The people complained about the harsh treatment they received from Solomon. They went on to say how they would serve Rehoboam faithfully if he would entreat them better.

Rehoboam requested three days to think it over. In that time he consulted with the elders of the nation to get their take on the situation. The elders advised him to entreat the people with fairness and earn their devotion.

After that, Rehoboam solicited the advice of his friends. Their instructions differed drastically from the older contemporaries. They advised Rehoboam to be extremely harsh with the people. They said, "If your father stung them with whips, you make them taste the sting of scorpions."

Rehoboam could not resist the peer pressure. Rather than gain the respect and love of the people, he chose to rule with an iron-clad fist. Rehoboam repeated the frightening forecast of his friends to the people and the result was devastating.

The harsh news divided the nation of Israel to this day and set them on a path to war that the Lord Himself had to stop. All of this could have been avoided if Rehoboam had the courage to say no to his friends.

This should be a lesson for us not to allow friends to dominate or dictate the outcomes of our lives. Never allow your friends to mistreat your spouse, your children or you in anyway.

When we can overcome the unrighteous influence of our friends the peace of God will rule our hearts. Please don't take this the wrong way, but some try to manipulate the relationship by asking things based upon friendship. Nepotism is not negative, but it could be used in a negative way.

Jesus was approached by James and John. These men were His disciples and His friends (Joh. 15:15). They chose to make a request of Jesus which had nothing to do with healing the sick or providing for the poor.

Jesus was teaching about God's kingdom and these brothers wanted to be kings. Jesus was planting spiritual seeds and they were plotting selfish schemes. Cowering behind their mother, she asked for them to be seated on the left and right side of Jesus as He ruled.

Jesus recognized their motives were not for ministry. These men thought they could manipulate based upon their friendship. Jesus was the Lamb of God, but they saw Him as a Cash Cow. Jesus was preparing for the cross and they were getting ready for their crowns. Not given to peer pressure, Jesus said no.

Saying no to family and friends is difficult, but it can be harder to say no to finances. Nevertheless, having the ability to say no to all of these is a prerequisite if we're to walk with God.

Saying No to Finances

There's nothing wrong with money. Although, many would contend with my view I hold fast to my confession. Some say money is the root of all evil, but this does not correlate with Scripture. The Bible says the *love* of money is the root to all evil (1st Tim. 6:10).

I've heard it said the *lack* of money is the root to all evil. Many probably would agree with that statement. In either case money is important and can be the answer to many of the world's problems (Eccl. 10:19).

Even though we need money, it should never become our motivation. If money becomes our motivation others will have the power to manipulate us with it. The Bible says we are tempted through lust *flesh etc.* (Jam. 1:14). Therefore, if we subtract lust we won't succumb to the traps the devil prepares for us.

The CEO of a company spoke with a female employee one evening. He complimented her work and offered a deal.

He asked, "Would you give yourself to me for $100,000?" The offer caught the woman totally off guard. She pondered the amount of money and then replied, "Yes, I would give myself to you for $100,000." He then asked, "Well, would you give yourself to me for $50,000."

The woman was upset that he reduced the sum, but figured his second offer was still a steep amount. Coincidently, she replied, "Yes, I would, for $50,000." The CEO looking to close the deal countered, "Ok, let's get down to business. Would you give yourself to me for $20.00?"

Infuriated the woman screamed, "What kind of woman do you think I am?" The man exclaimed, "We've already discovered what kind of woman you are; now we're just negotiating prices."

When we do not know how to say no to finances the devil will play us every time.

The Moabite king Balak summoned God's prophet Balaam. This king wanted to curse God's people, and he offered Balaam a substantial amount of money to do his bidding.

Balaam consulted with God about the offer which was his first offense. He preferred payment above God's people, God instructed him not to go with the Moabite king, but Balak made an offer Balaam could not refuse. *have J?*

Salivating over the salary he brought the king's second proposition back to God. The Lord was wroth due to Balaam's greed, but allowed him to accompany the king under divine guidance. Balaam was told that he could speak only what God commanded him to say.

Balaam's struggle with saying no to finances almost got him killed (Num. 22:33). The moral of Balaam's account is don't become a prophet for profit.

Being able to say no allows us to topple the fear of rejection. The Lord is our great reward. If we lose everything we own and all we have left is Him we have enough to start again. Also, if we lose everything and still have Jesus, He's more than enough.

When we fully comprehend the depth, breath and length of God's love for us, the fear of being rejected is irrelevant. My friend, know God loves you and accepts you because He made you. To know God's love is to unleash unlimited possibilities in your life.

Removing the fear of rejection removes the devils restrictions. Wherever you are, you've been empowered by God to go further. If you can believe it and conceive it; you will receive and achieve it.

Chapter Seven

Overcoming the Fear of Failure

Though he fall, he shall not be utterly cast down: for the Lord upholdeth him with his hand.

—Psalm 37:24

Why do some people achieve much in life while others remain underprivileged? Could it be opportunities are segregated by class, race, education, religion or any of the other social lines that divide society? Some would think so. They may argue there must be some force at play deciding the fate of all people.

Beyond social divides there's a fundamental factor that keep people from doing well. Many people never succeed because of the fear of failure.

These people would rather play it safe than to take any kind of risks. They settle for drifting through life rather than driving toward a designated goal. It's easy to drift, but driving takes focus; it takes faith.

The Lord wants us to live a life without limits; one filled with excitement. God offers immunity from the mundane; He's provided a route from the routine. There are times when ordinary should be secondary, and God's abundant living should be primary.

God needs us to succeed! When we are overcomers we are able to help others through their trials. For us to do well and excel we must overcome the fear of failure. To hurdle this feat takes understanding failure is not a flaw, it's not final or fatal.

Failure Is Not a Flaw

To say failure is not a flaw is to understand there's nothing wrong with failing. We all fail whether we want to or not. Regarding that, failure does not make us failures. Likewise, it's better to try and make a mistake than to make the mistake of not trying.

We should never act spineless because of the fear of failure. In fact, it's through failure we can gain a higher education. Failure presents us with the opportunity to grow in the knowledge of who God is and how far He is willing to go on our behalf.

Reared in Egypt and raised as the son of the Pharaoh, Moses was accustomed to the better things in life. He was nurtured in fine culture; elevated above his peers and educated in superior schools. He had everything going for him and lacked no advantages.

However, his destiny was not to be a dignitary in Egypt but a deliverer of Israel. Somewhere between adolescence and adulthood he discovered God's plan for his life. He appeared to be an Egyptian on the outside, but he was bona fide Hebrew on the inside. The Pharaoh raised him from a kid to a king. In contrast, God needed him to be an under-shepherd for His kids.

After watching an Egyptian whipping two of his Hebrew brothers, Moses felt the time to take action had arrived.

As a knee-jerk reaction Moses murdered a man. In a moment, he moved from the place of defender to offender and his Egyptian crown forever loss by this crime. He went from ruling to running. His failure caused him to flee.

The man who was accustomed to the forefront found himself on the backside. A man once famous was now infamous. Just as his fire went out, God's flame blazed with passion and purpose. Moses was thinking retirement; God was thinking reassignment.

The Lord instructed Moses to go and lead the people of Israel out of Egypt. Moses complained, "I'm only one man." God explained, "I created men." From the place of failure Moses asked, "Who am I?" From the place of success God answered, "I Am!"

The Lord is looking to do marvelous things in our lives, but He's going to need us to follow Him by faith. God has our success plan ensconced in His Word. If we read His Word and meditate on it day and night we will experience good success (Jos. 1:8). God is not looking to merely do things for us; He's looking to do things through us. He can bring us to our place of success if we get the right perspective about failure.

A little boy was playing with his bat and ball in the front yard as his mother watched through their living room window.

The mother witnessed her son throw his ball up in the air. Each time he threw the ball in the air he would yell out, "I'm the greatest hitter in the world." As the ball would reach eye level the boy would attempt to hit the ball with his bat. However, to no avail, he would miss.

The boy repeated this practice and every time he would yell, "I'm the greatest hitter in the whole world." Time after time he would miss. The mother watched with sad disappointment.

Finally, the boy entered the house with much enthusiasm. The mother was totally surprised so she asked, "Son why are you so happy? You never hit the ball." To this the son replied, "I thought I was the greatest hitter in the world, but discovered I'm the greatest pitcher in the world."

When we can fail and not see ourselves as failures it will serve as a prelude to our success. It may take failing in one area to discover our strength in another. Did you know God can use those who've failed and will use those who've failed because all have failed? The fact is, the Lord presents us faultless and gives us great joy (Jude 24).

As much as we must appreciate failure is not a flaw, we must comprehend it is not final.

Failure Is Not Final

When a baby is born he is unable to walk. Therefore a baby must be coddled and carried wherever he is taken. Invariably, the baby develops to the toddler stage. As a toddler, he doesn't automatically stand and walk. A toddler begins to toddle by wobbling and stumbling.

When taking his first steps he will stumble, fumble and inevitably fall. The toddler may consider his falling as failing. However, somewhere nearby is a proud parent. The parent knows the toddler fell, but the parent doesn't see failure, he or she recognizes this prelude to success.

A good parent helps the child by picking him up. Nevertheless, the toddler while learning to walk will wobble and fall down again and again. If the child is to succeed, the parent progresses from *picking-up* to *helping-up* the toddler. And the parent knows that eventually he will be *getting-up* by himself. Furthermore, if the parent continues to pick the toddler up every time he falls his fear of failure will be confirmed. The fact is, his ability to get up is indicative of the toddler's success.

God has built within every one of us the innate ability to get up again. He knows we're going to fall in life. Even still, He's aware that failure is not final; it's a stage for us to learn and eventually grow.

There's a process to progress and in the process we fall, we fail, but we must get up again in order to win. The Word of God reveals a just man falls seven times, but he gets back up again (Prov. 24:16).

The cards of life may be stacked against us and the odds not in our favor, but don't give up, just look up and get up. God shows up and shows us He is greater than our problems. His hands will straighten and strengthen us.

The Lord and His disciples were traveling to Galilee. The disciples were baptizing folk in Judea when Jesus concluded it was time to pack it in and head for home.

Along the way they crossed through a Samaritan village. Weary from the journey Jesus decided rest was in order. The disciples had their minds on lunch, but Jesus needed to extend His love. They had hungry stomachs, but Jesus was there to feed a hungry heart.

On the edge of town was a well and this would prove to be the perfect meeting place. It was there Jesus met a woman who knew failure first hand. She knew defeat like a fish knew water. However, she was on a collision course with her divine destiny.

Like a detective, Jesus probed through her personal life with precision. As a five-time wife, marriage for her was a miscarriage. Men picked her up only to let her down. And her letdowns made her feel lowdown. Her dreams of success were marred by disaster.

This woman was the walking dead, but Jesus was her Living Water. God made an appointment with her disappointment. She viewed failure as final and soon discovered it was the opportunity for God to make a radical change in her life. Her misery became her ministry. God took a woman with no class and moved her to the head of the class.

Once we truly accept failure as a part of progressing in life we won't become unglued when it happens. The devil desires to keep us fearing failure. He knows when we are afraid to fail our walk with God is hindered.

When we walk with God we are in a no-failing-zone, because it's impossible for Him to fail. This is simply to say, our perception of failure becomes a positive not a negative.

A person taking a class in English is given various tests throughout the course. Now, let's say the person received a failing grade on one of her test. Failing the test doesn't mean she failed the course. In essence, the failing grade on the test didn't predict the outcome of the course at all. Although this person received a failing test grade she can still pass the overall class.

So it is with life! We can fail in areas of our family, profession and finances, but it doesn't predict our future. No matter what, failure doesn't have to be final and it doesn't need to be fatal.

FAILURE IS NOT FATAL

An unemployed executive answered an intriguing job ad for the regional zoo. The human resources manager explained that the zoo's gorilla had died, and it was cheaper to hire someone to dress in a gorilla's suit than to get another gorilla. The man was desperate for a job, so he took it.

The first day wasn't too bad. He paced the floor, ate the peanuts and bananas thrown to him, and thumped on his chest. The next day, he became bolder and began swinging on the rope tied to an old tree. As he swung, he suddenly lost his grip and fell into the lion's den next door.

He jumped to his feet and began to scream, "Help! Help!" The lion came out of his cave to see what the commotion was all about, and then he pounced on the man in the gorilla suit and said, "Shhh, if you don't shut up, we'll both lose our jobs!"

In life we will fall. There will be times when our choices place us in compromising positions. However, every failure doesn't have to be fatal.

Some never excel in their profession because they fear jeopardizing their position. For fear of rocking the boat they allow their ship to sink. They fear destruction and therefore never have a hand in construction.

Going through life hoping to never fail is unrealistic. The Lord doesn't place that kind of demand on us. Therefore, we should not place that burden on ourselves. I'm not purporting we should strive to fail. I'm not even saying we should enjoy failing. Consequently, I am conveying we need to appreciate failure for what it is and not fear for what it is not.

Don't see failure as merely a mistake, but a measuring rod. I'll admit failure is not fun; but it doesn't have to be fatal. Even if it's self-imposed.

Jonah was given a mission from God. This obligation would call for his full participation, and cooperating was not what Jonah was willing to do.

The Ninevites were enemies of Israel. They killed men for sport and forced women into slavery. When noise from their pagan parties reached the halls of heaven, God decided they needed to repent or He would reprove.

The Lord instructed Jonah to preach to this wicked nation. Because Jonah disagreed with God's will, he decided to disregard God's word. Jonah deliberately boarded a ship headed in the opposite direction of God's assignment. His refusal brought God's retribution. Jonah's failure changed his fate.

God caused a violent storm to whip upon the ship. The vessel's passengers were stunned, but Jonah was stubborn. As the crew devised plans for survival; God was calling Jonah for revival. The crew sought to appease God's anger, but Jonah's failure to obey only angered God more.

Jonah's prejudice produced his prosecution. While he was contemplating death, God's plan called for life and not just Jonah's life, but the Ninevites as well. Jonah's failure earned him a three night stay in the belly of a fish. This fish ride would eventually break Jonah's pride. He learned a valuable lesson. Failure isn't fun, but it doesn't have to be fatal.

Beloved, the Lord has plans for you and they are plans for good and not evil. His heart is to see you succeed in life (Jer. 29:11). All you have to do is trust Him. Even when you can't see the outcome you should still follow the Lord.

The fear of failure has surfaced at one point or another in all our lives. However, we must overcome this fear. When we know that failure is not a flaw, it's not final or fatal we will move forward confidently.

The Lord waits just beyond the horizon and what He has for us will catapult us to another dimension of success. Do you want it? Overcome the fear of failure.

Chapter Eight
The Trapeze Act

Now unto him that is able to keep you from falling, and to present you faultless before the presence of his glory with exceeding joy...

—Jude 24

Having conquered the fear of failure allows us to walk with God in confidence. This confidence stems from knowing the Lord has our best interest at heart, and desires to elevate us from one level of faith to another. God needs us to trust Him. The analogy of a double trapeze act is a graphic depiction of this level of trust.

The double trapeze act is an amazing amusement for all to see. This performance was invented in 1859 by a Frenchman, Jules Leotard, who connected a bar to some ventilator cords above the swimming pool in his father's gymnasium. This amateur show involving two trapeze artists later became the spectacle it is today. This act consists of a catcher and a flyer.

The catcher hangs from a swinging bar by his knees and sends commands to the flyer. The catcher's responsibility as indicated by his title is to catch his partner. The flyer also swings from a moving bar. However, the flyer performs the maneuvers in the air and flies with grace and ease into the hands of the catcher.

The double trapeze act provides a picture of the way God operates with His people. According to the analogy, God is the Catcher and we are the flyers. Subtracting the fear of failure and maneuvering by faith is critical for success.

This remarkable feat is performed with precision. Moreover, the double trapeze act is fruitful when utilizing three main factors—ability, attitude and authority.

Trust God's Ability

In the double trapeze act all the attention is usually placed on the flyer. The flyer's flips and spins in the air are absolutely breath-taking. However, the success of the act greatly depends on the strength of the catcher. If the catcher's strength is in question, the flyer's confidence will diminish.

Likewise, our success depends on the strength of our Lord. His power enables us to soar through life. At times we might feel as though our lives are flipping upside down or spinning out of control, but this is far from the truth. The flipping and spinning is a part of the Catcher's plan. Remember no matter what, the Lord is in control.

During one of our prayer meetings a member of our church asked if we could pray about her condition. A couple of days prior to the meeting she had been diagnosed with cancer. Her physician detected the cancer and reported it was the size of a grapefruit.

This same doctor scheduled her for surgery to remove the mass. In the prayer meeting she acknowledged the problem, but quickly confessed her faith in God's power. We prayed and believed God for her healing.

At her follow-up appointment, her doctor was stunned

by the findings during the examination. The cancer had disappeared, so he quickly sought the opinion of a fellow physician. The second practitioner was baffled by the cancer's disappearance, also. Both men suspected their equipment had malfunctioned. Thus, they requested she be examined at an entirely different hospital. Coincidently, the medical staff of the second hospital surrendered the same results.

In amazement, the physicians have requested to use her case for future study. God cancelled the cancer! She is no longer preparing for surgery, instead she is being considered for medical research. God's power is greater than our problems!

When faced with problems and pressure, don't doubt God. The Bible records: Now unto him that is able to keep you from falling… (Jude 24). As the Catcher, the Lord's grip is tight and His touch gives us peace. Remember, our problems become an opportunity for God to show Himself strong on our behalf.

Every disappointment to us is literally an appointment with God. During problems we cry, "Lord, why now—Why me?" God says, "It's your time." "It's your turn." The Lord is not in the business of decreasing our problems; He wants to increase His power in us to handle the problems. More importantly, the Lord is looking to move us to the next level of faith. God has power to empower.

TRAIN OUR ATTITUDE

The double trapeze act is performed at great heights, and the high altitude is what sets it apart from other performances. In like manner, God operates from a heavenly perspective. His thoughts and ways are higher than ours (Isa. 55:9).

Connecting with God involves our willingness to go higher with Him. As the flyer, we aren't satisfied dwelling in the lowlands. Our fulfillment is discovered while soaring.

What would you accomplish if you could not fail? Where would you go if the world's limitations were lifted from your life? How would you perform if your critics were silenced?

Believe it or not, your attitude can cause the impossible to become possible. A person's attitude will either cause him to go higher or lower in life.

We were created to soar like an eagle. An eagle never complains about traffic because it soars above the common fray of everyday negativity.

The term, "Your attitude determines your altitude" is profound and true. This is an aeronautical term to define a concept used by pilots. Inside the cockpit of an aircraft you may find what is called an ***Attitude Indicator***. The attitude indicator shows the aircraft's position in relation to the earth's horizon.

In fact, it is said when the nose of the aircraft is up the attitude of the plane is high and when the nose is down the attitude is low. The same can be said regarding people. God has built within each of us attitude indicators to help direct our noses. When our nose is up we look-up and depend on God. In contrast, a downward nose indicates we have lost our hope. Thus, aiming high begins with our attitude.

A man was watching a little league baseball game. In the first inning the visiting team was beating the home team by a score of 18-0. Hoping the home team would win the man became discouraged.

In disgust, he packed his belongings and prepared to leave. A little boy who was also rooting for the home team asked the man why he was leaving the game so soon. Surprised the man responded, "Can't you see the score? It's just the 1st inning and the visiting team is beating the pants off us." The boy smiled and said, "Yeah, but our team hasn't gotten a chance to bat yet."

When we possess the right attitude we'll remove the word quit from our vocabulary. When it appears trouble is ahead, just wait, God is about to turn the table and the score will be in our favor. In life you may have gotten knocked down, but you're not knocked out. Just because a door is shut, it doesn't mean the door is locked. The right attitude can overcome any obstacle.

The blind brought only their belief. The deaf defied despair and the dumb dared not be denied. Among the deprived and desperate was a cripple without crutches. The only common thread among the diseased and destitute was their hope for healing.

God chose a pool to reveal His power. This was the season He would send salvation. This was the place God would move the water in order to mend. No one challenged His way they just waited for Him to work.

The cripple lay impotent for thirty-eight years. For this reason, Jesus confronted him concerning his condition. The cripple complained about his position, but Jesus enquired of his disposition. Jesus asked the man, "Do you want to be healed?" In essence, Jesus was inferring his attitude determined his altitude.

The cripple's *attitude indicator* was in the negative. Therefore, the man's negative mind gave him a negative mood, which ultimately negated his move. However, by a simple attitude adjustment the cripple progressed from weak to well. And, he was able to carry the bed that once carried him.

Our attitude will make us victors or victims; it is the difference between operating in faith or conceding to failure.

Trace God's Authority

There's a final element to the trapeze act that needs to be discussed. This element is the catcher's authority. The catcher is responsible for signaling the flyer. Consequently, the flyer must be sensitive to the catcher's signals or the performance can be disastrous.

Again, God is always the Catcher and we must trace His authority. To trace God is to pursue or come after Him with a passion. Many people *come to* the Lord, but fail to *come after* Him (Lu. 14:26-27). To come to the Lord means to accept His deliverance. However, to come after the Lord is to follow His directions.

Mark it down; the flyer's refusal to follow the Catcher's directions results in failure. The Catcher enables the flyer to execute mid-air maneuvers because He is there as support. Without the Catcher the act is impossible.

In the trapeze act it is paramount for the flyer to touch the catcher throughout the performance, but even more critical is their timing. God's will is always connected to His timing.

Joshua was proven in battle and his name was synonymous with victory. His enemies regretted the day they crossed his path and his God. Suddenly he stood before his greatest challenge—Jericho.

Jericho was a monumental metropolis. It's beauty only overshadowed by its bars. This city boasted vast fortune and bragged that it was fortified. Jericho was widely considered the Fort Knox of its day.

While Joshua was sizing Jericho's walls, the Lord was seizing Joshua's will. God revealed His rank as Captain and Commander and Joshua surrendered as His servant. Joshua asked the Lord to take sides, but God took over.

The defeat of Jericho was God's will, but it could only occur through God's timing. God instructed Joshua and Israel to walk and not talk for six days. However, on the seventh day they were to circle Jericho seven times and then shout. When Israel cried the walls cracked. Jericho's tragedy became Israel's triumph. When we obey God's authority we'll experience His victory.

Allowing God to direct us will ensure our success. He is the Great, Good, and Chief Shepherd who leads us to green pastures. Nevertheless, we ought not become discouraged by the way He leads us. At times, God will lead us through some valleys. On occasions, He will take us up the rough side of the mountain. Rest assured; His ways are for our benefit not detriment.

We must trace His authority and not permit detours to deter our attitude on this journey of life. God's direction may not be the preferred way, but it is the perfect way. Jesus said His sheep know His voice and the voice of a stranger they will not follow (John 10:27). The more sensitive we are to His voice the better our chances of success.

Operating in God's authority releases His ability. Ensconced in every command of God is His promise of victory. Understand, God does not promise prevention from adversity; He promises protection through adversity.

Therefore, we must trust in the Catcher's ability and authority. And, as the flyer we need to train our attitude to determine our altitude. Then, we will soar without limits.

Part Two

Thou shalt tread upon the lion and adder: the young lion and the dragon shalt thou trample under feet.

Psalm 91:13 kjv

Chapter Nine
Overcoming the Fear of the Lion
"Backtalk the Devil"

> Who through faith subdued kingdoms, wrought righteousness, obtained promises, **stopped the mouths of lions**...
>
> —Hebrews 11:33

As the sun sets in its rightful place, the cooling winds of the evening begin covering the land and settling the beasts of the region. For the vast majority of creatures the day has ended, but for the lioness, the day has just begun.

The antelope play blissfully in ignorance and are comforted by the calmness of the stream. Water quietly trickles quenching the thirst of the herd. The skies are filled with birds searching for a place to rest during the African night. The antelope raise their heads frequently surveying the outback to determine if the scene is safe.

However, in the silence, beyond the shadows, and nestled in tall blades of grass, lurks the largest member of the feline family. She is camouflaged by the very territory for which she has dominion. What she lacks in speed, is found abundantly in intelligence, precision and patience.

From a distance the lioness spots the antelope. Her claws dig into the earth as she pinpoints the game. Her eyes light up in the moonlight, deep breaths are taken as her senses are enhanced. The moment is intense as the antelope's next move is anticipated.

The lioness is focused on the meal. With head and nose to the ground, body low, she maneuvers undetected one step at a time. Far enough to remain concealed yet close enough to smell her prey, the lioness waits for opportunity.

In an instance, the winds cease, and for a split second the antelope attempt their escape. Impulsively, with a great charging roar, the lioness raises and rushes the herd. Its roar reverberates from every corner of the canyon and confuses its victims. The roar causes panic and for some paralysis. This night another life is lost.

This opening vignette reveals the hunting style of the lioness, as well as the devious technique of the devil.

The Apostle Peter describes the devil as a roaring lion (1st Pet. 5:8). His depiction of Satan gives insight to his duplicitous dealings. Like the lioness that relies upon her ferocious roar to instill fear in her potential prey, the devil rouses our fear through what we hear.

People are often fearful because of negative reports. The evening newscasters announce the world's economic crisis and climbing gasoline prices. Stories are told of foreign plots to attack various countries, and there are insufficiencies with Homeland security.

If the devil is roaring one negative report after another, there is one way to cage this cat. We must roar back! In other words, we must backtalk the devil. We can't allow the enemy or our circumstances to have the final word.

God has given us a vocabulary. Whenever we are behind enemy lines, His language brings victory. This vocabulary comprises three elements which repel the roar of the lion that threatens to paralyze our faith.

The Vocabulary of Scripture

The worlds were framed by the word of God (Heb. 11:3). Think about that for a second. God created the worlds and then He caused them to be sustained in place by the word He spoke.

Our planet was on a downward spiral of disarray. It was active in an abyss and engulfed in utter darkness. Then God decided restoration was in order. His reconstruction plan did not call for any heavy operating equipment. He didn't use a crane to align the stars. The mountains weren't plowed in place by a bulldozer, nor the oceans restocked by a dump truck. All He needed to restore this world was His word.

The same can be said concerning our world today. The Lord cares about our personal lives. He desires to see us succeed in all areas. Therefore, He has given us the very element He used to restore and revive—His Word.

If your life is unproductive begin speaking what the Scriptures declare about you.

A young man asked an old rich man how he made his fortune. The old guy looked the lad in his eyes and said, "Well, son, it was 1932, in the depth of the Great Depression. I was down to my last nickel and I invested it in an apple. I spent the entire day polishing the apple, and then sold it for ten cents. With the ten cents I bought two apples, polished them and sold them for twenty cents. I continued this process and by the end of the month I accumulated a fortune of $1.40."

Then the old guy paused, removed his eye glasses,

wiped them clean, looked the young man back in his eyes and said, "Then my wife's father died and left us two million dollars."

Like that two million dollars, God's word can change our situation immediately. Many are frustrated because they are trying to figure out what only God can work out. God's word supersedes man's skill. It goes beyond man's ability, and exceeds man's knowledge. Most importantly, God's word defeats the devil.

Jesus was led into the desert to faceoff with the devil. After His forty day fast, He was tuned into holiness, but tapped out from hungriness. Looking to take advantage of what he thought was prey, the devil tipped in to tempt Him. Not sure of the Lord's identity, the devil tested Jesus' divinity.

The lion roared, "Turn these stones into bread!" Jesus back-talked the devil, and quoted Scripture. The devil was offering bread, however Jesus was not given to bribes.

Jesus was led a second time, but this time the spirit was not divine, it was demonic. Jesus found Himself on the temple with the tempter. Breathing challenges, the devil dared, but the Lord denied. While Lucifer was lurking in the wind, the Lord was leaning on the Word.

The lion roared, "Jump!" Again, Jesus back-talked the devil, He let the Word work. The devil wanted Jesus to fall, but the Scriptures allowed Jesus to take His stand.

Sweltering from rejection and pacing like a panther, the devil offered Jesus kingdoms without recognizing he was talking to the King. Again Jesus back-talked the enemy and by saying what was written He turned a lion into a kitten.

Whenever face to face with the enemy, use the vocabulary of scripture and see the feline flee.

THE VOCABULARY OF SILENCE

There's an old adage that says, "Actions speak louder than words." There are times when it's not good to speak at all. When you receive bad news, fear grips your heart, and you don't know what to say—don't say anything. When a disagreement has the possibility to escalate to a full scale verbal war, before you give a piece of your mind—put your mouth on mute.

I learned long ago when confusion progresses to frustration to turn my station to K.Y.M.S (Keep Your Mouth Shut). The devil doesn't know what you're thinking until you tell him. He lies low, lurking, listening and once you reveal your vulnerability he lunges to attack.

God gives strength and power unto His people (Ps. 68:35) therefore; you don't have to fear the devil. Many ask for God's strength without fully comprehending the way His strength is obtained. His strength is not delivered to you, it's developed within you.

In order to appreciate God's gifts of strength and power you must differentiate between the two. Strength is what you have on the inside as a result of what is taking place on the outside. Power is what's displayed on the outside as a result of what you have on the inside.

If strength is developed, there must be external pressures. In life you will hear negative reports and even experience hardships. It's in these moments you discover tough times don't last, but tough people do. The devil is like a lion, but God is the Lion Tamer. The Word of God admonishes, be slow to speak (Jas. 1:19). Many times holding your peace will keep you from falling to pieces.

As the summer was coming to an end, a flock of birds were planning to fly south. A frog asked if he could go with them. The birds questioned how the frog could join the flight because frogs are unable to fly. The frog suggested two birds hold opposite ends of a rope in their beaks while he would hold onto the middle with his mouth. They all agreed the idea was great, so they put the plan into effect.

The birds and frog were spotted while flying over a town. Someone quickly yelled, "Look, there's a frog flying between two birds." Another person asked, "I wonder who thought of that unique idea?" Not wanting to miss an opportunity for recognition, the frog opened his mouth and said, "I diiiiiid."

✱ There will be times when opening your mouth will cause more harm than good. God is looking to reveal His power and sometimes talking can thwart His work. There are seasons when the vocabulary of silence is all that's needed.

The times were harsh and the town lacked help. A famine was within the walls while a foe waited without. Like trash, four men were thrown outside the city gate. These four found themselves discouraged and diseased. The Bible doesn't mention their names only their conditions.

The scorching sun cooked their carcasses. Their stomachs empty of substance and their hearts empty of hope. Good health was a distant memory and wealth was a dream deferred. Devoid of family and facing a dismal future, these four heard the lion's roar.

"Your health is going from bad to worse. You'll die of starvation. The enemy is only hours away." As they sat surely they must have thought soon someone will save us. However, the hours progressed to days and no one came—no one cared.

Just when the lion thought he had them, they decided complaining wasn't going to solve the situation so they walked. No one spoke a word they just walked.

As these four men walked in a direction God took them to a new dimension. Although feeble, they walked by faith.

As they shuffled weary feet and worn-out legs toward the enemy God caused a sound to be heard for miles and miles. The four men barely heard their thoughts, but the enemy heard God's thunder. While the four practiced the vocabulary of silence, God created the kind of special effects that would cause George Lucas' head to spin.

Their ending was better than their beginning. They instantly went from rags to riches. They went from being lepers to overcoming the leopard. Their actions spoke louder than their words.

When bad news arrives let the cat think he's got your tongue. The truth is through the vocabulary of silence, the devil thinks you're in fear when you're actually in faith—<u>let silence stifle the enemy's strategy.</u>

THE VOCABULARY OF SIGN

Before the days of GPS (Global Positioning Systems) I relied on my navigational skills when driving long distances. I'll admit whenever traveling I found comfort seeing signs indicating the city was ahead. The signs were welcomed with relief and a resolve to continue driving toward my destination.

Signs serve as warnings and reminders. They can be used for advertisement and advisement. Above all, signs give direction to the otherwise misdirected, they set the course for those who veer off course.

The <u>vocabulary of scripture</u> and the <u>vocabulary of silence delineate how we communicate</u>; while the <u>vocabulary of sign describes how God communicates.</u> Throughout scripture we find <u>God communicating through signs</u>.

The word sign is the root word in signature. In essence, when <u>God gives us His sign He is writing His signature</u>. The Lord led Israel to the promise land by signs. He told them to follow the pillar of cloud by day and the pillar of fire by night (Ex. 13:21).

We are living in troublesome times, but there's no need to be troubled. Just as God was a sign then, He is a sign now. When the lion roars and rumors rise allow God's signs to be your guide.

The most memorable sign God gave was the rainbow, which guarantees flood protection. When it seems as though we're in over our heads, when the enemy comes in like a flood, we must remember God promised to lift up a standard of protection (Isa. 59:19). The signs He gives encourage us not to forfeit what He says is rightfully ours.

Abraham and Sarah were without an heir to carry on their name. Therefore, Abraham sought the Lord for a successor. Touched with compassion, God said He would grant His old friend's request. Abraham was elated with the news of his heir. Afterwards, Abraham heard a roar.

The first roar came from the direction of his wife when she chuckled at the concept of a child. The subsequent roars came with the passing of each birthday. Abraham began thinking he was too old and God was too late. God ensured Abraham that His delay didn't mean denial.

Abraham was awaiting a child, but God was preparing him for children. Abraham requested a son, but God was sowing seeds. God was giving Abraham time to gather strength before He demonstrated His power. Hearing His friend's sigh, God decided it was time for a sign.

In the day God asked Abraham to number the sand and in the night God instructed him to count the stars. The Lord said just as the sand and stars so shall your sons be—innumerable. Abraham was given direction and deliverance through the vocabulary of God's signs.

Beloved, be patient for God's promise. When you're

81

down to nothing, God is up to something. His sign language reveals His power and presence. And what He promises He is fully capable of performing (Rom. 4:21).

Overcome the fear of the lion through the vocabulary of scripture, silence and sign. The next time you hear the lion's roar, remember, it doesn't mean the threat is real.

Chapter Ten
Fix Your Heart

My heart is fixed, O God, **my heart is fixed**: I will sing and give praise.

—Psalm 57:7

The skies were clear, the winds calm and the aircraft's instruments were performing perfectly. Having received his clearance from the tower the pilot was confident the flight would be successful. However, his confidence and experience would soon be tested.

Suddenly the blue skies darkened. The calm flight was abruptly interrupted with violent turbulence. The pilot found himself in the midst of a storm. Rain pelted on the windshield of the cockpit causing poor visibility. A novice would have reason to panic, but this seasoned aviator was no novice.

He radioed his current status to the nearest tower. The tower personnel assured him they were monitoring the situation and the inclement weather was set to pass. The aircraft's instruments and directions from the tower allowed the pilot to navigate through the storm.

Like the pilot in this illustration we must have the ability to navigate through the storms of life because trouble visits us all. As the pilot relies on the aircraft's instruments and the experience of the tower personnel, we must depend on the Lord and His Word. The Word of God informs us that the name of the Lord is a strong tower in which the righteous find refuge (Prov. 18:10). Successful navigation occurs when our hearts are fixed, trusting in the Lord.

Fear can cause us to lose focus. Through fear we can forget our God is great and even more importantly how good He is. He has the power to defeat any opponent we might face. And, His goodness works toward our advantage in any adverse situation. In light of this, the operative command is when you lose focus stay fixed.

> He shall not be afraid of evil tidings: his heart is fixed, trusting in the Lord. His heart is established, he shall not be afraid, until he see his desire upon his enemies.
>
> —Psalm 112:7-8

God has destined each of us for success. Our success is not predicated upon fair weather or favorable conditions. Our success depends solely upon trusting God's plan for our life and allowing Him to develop us to fulfill that plan. Having our hearts fixed to trust the Lord doesn't happen naturally, there is a process.

TRAIN YOUR HEART TO BELIEVE

Nowadays believing in anything can be difficult? Unbelief can occur because of the world's view, and getting people to believe in God can be extremely arduous. Despite the world's pessimism, skepticism, and nihilism, we can train our hearts to believe. Although life throws one letdown after another, it's vital to understand God will never let us down.

The Lord expects us to live up in a down world; to be good in a bad world; and to be light in a dark world. Through faith we train our hearts to believe God's Word and obey His way. Whether high or low, on mountains or in valleys, we trust God's way is best. The problem for many is not the absence of faith, but rather the object of faith.

A man can have great faith, leap on thin ice and fall right through. Even still, another man can have little faith, tiptoe on thick ice and never fall through. The point of emphasis is not their faith; it's the object of their faith. When Jesus is the object of our faith failure is not an option.

Think about it, over half of what we believe came from another source as oppose to first-hand knowledge. Therefore, it becomes vitally important to guard our hearts. We must train our hearts to believe the Word of God so we won't believe the negative reports of the world.

This world is filled with many voices. John the Baptist said, "I am the voice of *one* crying in the wilderness (John 1:23)." This gives credence to the fact that there are other voices. However, it is up to us to determine which voice we will believe. The angels of God obey the voice of the Word (Ps. 103:20). Of course it makes good sense for us to do the same. However, before we can obey the voice of the Word we must believe the Word.

The Word of God is like an unknown chemical composition. It's necessary for our spiritual enrichment and edification. We can't grow or go without it!

An Army Airborne Ranger was learning to parachute. His Sergeant barked the orders:

1. Jump when you are told to jump.

2. Count to ten, and pull the rip cord.

3. If the first chute doesn't open, pull the second rip cord.

4. When you land, a truck will take you back to the post.

When the plane got over the landing zone, the soldier jumped when it was his turn. He counted to ten, and pulled the rip cord. Nothing happened. He pulled the second rip cord. Still, nothing happened. "Oh great," he complained to himself. "I'll bet the truck won't be waiting for me either."

God gives us instructions for our lives. However, to obtain success we must follow His instructions implicitly. And when it appears that nothing is happening, remember God is up to something. Our belief in His Word causes our hearts to become fixed, trusting that His way is better than our own.

The devil doesn't care that we hear the Word, but he is terrorized by those who hear the Word of God, believe, and act on the Word they hear. When we believe the Word of God, act on what we believe, we'll see our enemies scattered and our desires fulfilled.

Training our hearts to believe God's Word opens the door to a life without limits. Jesus told a desperate man all things are possible to them that believe (Mark 9:23). Imagine that, we can move from the realm of impossible to all-things-are-possible when we believe God's Word.

Teach Your Mouth What to Speak

There are many closet Christians today. These are people who neglect to vocalize their faith in God. Therefore, they acquiesce to negative circumstances hoping for relief in silent belief. Fear is everywhere and the only way to dispel fear is through faith in the living God. Consequently, we must speak what we believe.

If we are to have God's best we must confess God's Word. The Bible instructs the weak to say they're strong (Joel 3:10). It doesn't say for the weak to say, "I'm not weak" that would be lying. Instead, the scripture encourages the weak to confess their belief and eventually through the power of God, possess what they confess.

Consider the following instructions from Jesus:

> Fear them not therefore: for there is nothing covered, that shall not be revealed; and hid, that shall not be known.
>
> What I tell you in darkness, that speak ye in light: and what ye hear in the ear, that preach ye upon the housetops.
>
> —Matt. 10:26-27

We must speak what God speaks! Today more than ever before, we must hold fast to the profession of our faith without doubting. Doubting is the Achilles heel to an ever-increasing faith. It causes us to question God's integrity and fidelity. Above all, doubting causes us to remain silent when the situation calls for us to speak the Word of God.

We must stand on the warranty and authority of Who God is and the Word He gives. No matter what obstacle we face we must believe God's power is greater than our problems. The power of God is His word. By His word the worlds were formed and set in place (Heb. 11:3). Through that same word our individual worlds, those things that matter and are out of place, will be structured and restored.

God's ability to succeed is greater than our own inability to fail. I believe this and personally live by it in every given situation. Having God's Word is better than man's warranty.

Is there some goal that seems out of reach? There is a way to obtain the unthinkable and gain the impossible. The dream that seems far-out is not out of sight. If you can see it and say it, you can have it.

God promised Israel the land of Canaan. However,

upon arriving there Israel discovered it was occupied by giants. Moses sent twelve spies to case the place and return with a report.

Ten spies returned with a negative report. They complained about being incapable of displacing the inhabitants. Two spies returned with a positive report. They celebrated God's ability to do what they were incapable of doing. Fortunately, God agreed with the two. Somehow the two understood what the ten missed—what God doesn't mention, doesn't matter.

God did not mention the giants because to Him they were midgets. What the ten viewed as too big to defeat, God was more than able to deflate. Joshua and Caleb recognized the bigness of their God. These men lived longer than any others in their generation. Because they believed God's word, and spoke the word they believed, they were able to see God's promise come to pass.

Authentic faith lives off the promises of God. Caleb's belief took him beyond the mundane to claiming his mountain. This man carried the word of God until that same word carried him. Can you imagine asking God for Mount Fuji? Even more, can you contemplate God granting your request? God gave Caleb His word and Caleb held God to it by speaking the same word God gave.

By teaching our mouths to speak God's Word we make the power of God available to accomplish our dreams and dispel our fears. Those who only talk about their fears cause their fears to reappear. God has given His Word for every situation in life. His Word is designed to infuse us with faith. Through faith our fears are diminished and our destiny is discovered.

Transform Your Mind to Think

The outcome of a person's life depends greatly on the income of that person's thinking concerning faith and facts.

A fact is information about circumstances or things that exist. The world views facts as final. Nevertheless, a fact should never have final authority for the child of God.

Facts are important, but they're not relevant for God to operate in our lives. Interestingly enough, the word *fact* is not written anywhere within the King James Holy Bible. The reason for the exclusion is simple. God operates through faith not facts. Having faith is far more important than having facts. Truth is—our faith changes facts! Amen!

Thinking *faith* over *fact* positions us to see God perform miracles. When we read and rehearse God's Word, His will is revealed and we can receive His very best.

The book of Joshua reveals as we meditate on the Word of God we shall meet with good success (Jos. 1:8). This word meditate carries a compound meaning. It denotes thinking inwardly and speaking outwardly.

For as he thinketh in his heart, so is he...

—Proverbs 23:7

It is encumbered upon us to think on the Word of God if we are to reach our maximum potential. In other words, we must think for a change. Do you desire to have a better life? If so, check your thought life.

Meditating on God's Word causes it to take root in our hearts, establishes faith in our lives and dismisses fear. Mark it down, where the Word of God is missing; the life of God is nonexistent.

Jesus emphatically proclaimed man must live on every word that proceeds out of the mouth of God (Matt. 4:4). By using the term *proceeds out of the mouth of God*, Jesus was alluding to what is considered the *engrafted word*. The engrafted word is the word we hear or read before the storms of life hit. Transforming our minds to think on God's engrafted word prepares and empowers us for any storm.

A foolish notion is thinking life will never present problems, pain or pressure. This concept is deluded and only makes matters worse. When storms occur we better be ready or fear will grip our hearts and rip our homes apart.

Transforming our minds to think faith over fact can move us from poverty to prosperity; hopelessness to hopefulness; and creates calm in the midst of chaos.

Jesus' mother Mary was asked to coordinate a wedding. The event had a confluence of fine dining and stimulating conversation. The guest list was entwined with the communities' popular and political.

Just as the evening was reaching its apex Mary was delivered alarming news. Requests for wine were in, but the wine reserve was out. Making matters worse, the governor was ready to give a toast to a full party with an empty glass.

Now the fact was not in Mary's favor. However, in spite of the fact she had a focused faith. She directed the servants to follow the directions of the Savior. Jesus instructed them to deliver water to a crowd that craved wine. The result was nothing short of remarkable.

The fact stated the wine was gone, but faith saw Jesus there. Mary relied on God's power and received the governor's praise. Her faith changed the fact!

Like Mary, we must train our minds to think of every situation as an opportunity for a miracle. We must think for a change!

Finally, brethren, whatsoever things are true, whatsoever things are honest, whatsoever things are just, whatsoever things are pure, whatsoever things are lovely, whatsoever things are of good report; if there be any virtue, and if there be any praise, think on these things.

—Philippians 4:8

Beloved, it is imperative that our hearts are fixed trusting in the Lord. Unfortunately, our society is saturated in sin and suffocating with sickness. Fear is everywhere but it doesn't have to dominate our lives.

God's Word is a defense in a world that is defiant. We can overcome this world's negative gravitational pull by training our hearts to believe, teaching our mouths what to speak and transforming our minds to think.

When times are tough; days are dark; and it becomes difficult to focus, remember to keep your heart fixed. The Lord is the Tower. He sees your condition and He's always in control.

Chapter Eleven

Overcoming the Fear of the Serpent

> Be not afraid of **sudden fear**, neither of the desolation of the wicked, when it cometh.
>
> —Proverbs 3:25

Looking at something dreadful can cause fear, and I refer to this as the serpent's fear. It occurs suddenly! Note, serpents slither and slide undetected; without warning they cause panic and paralysis. Likewise, the devil attempts to instill panic in his victims. He cunningly uses seen catastrophes to produce sudden fear in our hearts.

Contrary to Satan's ploy, the Lord has not given us the spirit of fear. He desires that we walk in confidence and the Scripture reveals we please our Father by faith (Heb. 11:6).

Neglecting to place our faith in the living God can allow the serpent's fear to appear. When we focus on distress, desolation and destruction, the devil perpetuates all kinds of phobias. Nevertheless, God's divine assurance can cause triumph over every tragedy.

> When your fear cometh as *desolation*, and your *destruction* cometh as a whirlwind; when *distress* and anguish cometh upon you. Then shall they call upon me, but I will not answer; they shall seek me early, but they shall not find me: For that they hated knowledge, and did not choose the fear of the Lord.
>
> —Proverbs 1:27-29 italics added

The Serpent's Fear of Distress

> And let us arise, and go up to Bethel; and I will make there an alter unto God, who answered me in the day of my *distress*, and was with me in the way which I went.
> —Genesis 35:3

"Mayday, Mayday, Mayday" is an international distress call used primarily by mariners and aviators. The call is made when the integrity of a vessel is being severely challenged. The word distress literally means to cause mental anguish or physical pain. It also carries the connotation to pull apart that which is meant to remain together. The devil's strategy is to disunite us from our Lord. Therefore, he manipulates distressful circumstances hoping to catch us in a vulnerable state.

Like a mariner or aviator, we too can send a distress call to God with the assurance of knowing He hears, and will answer.

> While we look not at the things which are seen, but at the things which are not seen: for the things which are seen are temporal; but the things which are not seen are eternal.
>
> —2 Corinthians 4:18

When circumstances look bleak, we can blink. In others words, we can ignore any situation that doesn't line up with the Word of God. Why give negative circumstances our full attention? They are subject to change anyway.

The Word of God instructs us to look at the things which <u>are not</u> seen. This directive implies there must be some <u>"unseen" things.</u> It's like an x-ray machine. The x-ray allows us to see things that are not seen (internal organs). These are things the naked eye cannot detect. Just like the x-ray, God allows us to see eternal things.

In the bible Joseph had the uncanny ability to look at negative situations in a positive way. Although he caught one bad break after another he was able to see light at the end of every dark tunnel. His paradigm was set toward the positive whenever he was presented with a negative.

He was beloved by his father and belittled by his brothers. They despised and denounced him. They plotted to kill him, but eventually decided merchandise was better than murder. Therefore, they bartered Joseph for money.

Joseph was snatched from security and forced into slavery. However, *God was with him*. Despite his captivity, Joseph didn't use his bondage as a bandage. Rather than succumbing to humiliation he served his master with humility. For that, he was given the chance to be in charge.

Just as things were looking up, his course took a downward spin. Joseph was wrongfully accused and placed in prison. Nevertheless, *God was with him*. Though caged he remained encouraged. And, in prison he was promoted.

Eventually Joseph's positive disposition brought his pardon. His God-given statutes earned him status. In the end, Joseph faced his brothers with the power to take their lives. Remarkably, he chose revival over revenge. His kindness was not due to an oversight, but rather insight.

Joseph informed his brothers that their evil deed was ultimately used in God's divine plan. In essence, his distress was an opportunity for God to bless.

The Serpent's Fear of Desolation

> For we were bondmen; yet our God hath not forsaken us in our bondage, but hath extended mercy unto us in the sight of the kings of Persia, to give us a reviving, to set up the house of our God, and to repair the *desolations* thereof, and to give us a wall in Judah and in Jerusalem.
>
> —Ezra 9:9

With the attributes of a serpent, the devil will attempt to use desolation to cause despair. However, we never need to operate out of desperation. Our God is great and mighty to save.

If we look back at the account with Joseph, we'll discover he was in a place of desolation. Desolation is considered a desert place; a forsaken place; a place of abandonment.

Joseph was in a dark pit, abandoned by those he trusted to protect him—his brothers. They abhorred him because of his God-inspired dream and threw him in a pit with the purpose of killing it.

Beloved, we must understand, the devil doesn't have the power to take our lives, but if we allow him; he will take over. He will use the serpent's fear of desolation to convince us that no one cares. However, this is not true. God truly loves and cares for us!

God promised He would never leave or abandon us (Heb. 13:5). Throughout Joseph's horrific ordeal the Scripture reminds us that *God was with him* (Gen. 39:2, 21). As God was with Joseph, He will accompany us during every desolate situation. It doesn't matter through divorce, indebtedness or even in death; God wants to remain the personal influence and strength of our lives.

One morning a farmer discovered his donkey had fallen into a six foot pit. Having no means by which to retrieve his donkey, he decided to fill the hole with dirt and count his losses.

As he shoveled dirt into the hole, the donkey would kick and fuss. However, with dirt on his back, the donkey decided this would not be his end. Every time the farmer threw dirt in the hole, the donkey would shake it off and pack it under his feet. Eventually, the donkey stepped out of the pit.

Remember, the dirt the devil uses for our burial plot, God uses in our planting pot. In essence, God can create life out of dirty situations; while the devil uses desolation as a distraction to remove our focus from the Main Attraction (Jesus).

> ARISE, SHINE; for thy light is come, and the glory of the LORD is risen upon thee. For, behold, the darkness shall cover the earth, and gross darkness the people: but the LORD shall arise upon thee, and his glory shall be seen upon thee.
>
> —Isaiah 60:1-2

When sudden fear tries to bombard our hearts, we must remember the Word of God. Even in a pit we should not become pitiful. When things look bad, we are instructed to look at Jesus Who is the Author and Finisher of our faith (Heb. 12:2).

THE SERPENT'S FEAR OF DESTRUCTION

> Pride goeth before *destruction*, and an haughty spirit before a fall.
>
> —Proverbs 16:18

Throughout this chapter we've been discovering how the devil looks to suppress us through the serpent's fear of what we see. Before we conclude, I want to discuss a covert tactic. The most deceptive scheme the devil uses against us is our own pride.

Through pride we can cause trouble in our lives that otherwise would not occur. Even more so, we can experience destruction of some sort and our pride prohibits us from seeking help. This reminds me of a saying, <u>"Anger can get us in trouble; but pride can keep us there."</u>

At one point the devil held a high position within the ranks of celestial beings. However, the bible records that he desired to promote himself above all of God's creation and ultimately God Himself (Isa. 14:12-14). Eventually, he was banished from heaven and demoted to his current demonic state.

For this reason, his plan is to bring destruction to all of God's people. Since he drives the vehicle of pride, it behooves us not to become his passengers.

King Nebuchadnezzar ruled Babylon from 562 to 605 B.C. His empire was vast and his power revered. He conquered many nations and placed their lands under Babylonian rule. Once he reached the pinnacle of success he allowed pride to get the best of him.

His arrogance progressed to ignorance. Before long this king began thinking he was above God. The only thing he valued more than his region was his reputation. And his reputation along with his life was headed for destruction.

Nebuchadnezzar was reduced from majesty to madness. He went from residing in the palace to eating in the pasture. He ate grass as a daily meal and his hair grew as a lion's mane. Like an animal, he roamed the countryside, his hands and feet were covered with claws. He became rumored and ridiculed, a catchphrase for all to caution.

Pride brought this king to pity, and humiliation took him to humility. Eventually, his broken state produced a broken spirit. Then, he was ready to acknowledge God. Once Nebuchhadnezzar recognized God as the Chief Umpire, God restored his empire.

The point is simple, <u>we must not allow the sin of pride to have place in our lives.</u> If we do, destruction is inevitable. If we happen to find ourselves in the midst of destruction, we mustn't fear because God will allow us to recover. There is an interesting and true story that describes this very fact.

In 1873 California was booming in the grape industry. Unfortunately, the state suffered a devastating drought which literally dried all the grapes on their vines. Those whose livelihood depended upon the grapes were fearful they would not be able to survive such destruction.

When the owners of the vineyards saw their crops destroyed they succumbed to the serpent's fear and practically gave up hope. However, one man had hopes of recouping in spite the misfortune. As an enterpriser, he sold the dried and shriveled grapes as a "Peruvian Delicacy." His insight and ingenuity literally catapulted the California raisin into a money making industry. See, during sudden fear God can bring production out of the devil's destruction.

When facing distress, desolation or destruction don't fret, have faith, knowing the Lord will overthrow the devil's plan and bring triumph out of each tragedy.

Because our eyes are on Jesus, we shall recover all.

Chapter Twelve
Get the Picture

> And he answered, Fear not: for they that be with us are more than they that be with them. And Elisha prayed, and said, LORD, I pray thee, **open his eyes that he may see**...
>
> —2nd Kings 6:16-17

The proper way to combat the serpent's fear is not to focus on negative visions, but rather set our sights on the Lord's positive plan for our lives.

It becomes paramount for us to comprehend that God desires the best for us. Armed with this picture, we are enabled to resist the devil when he attempts to paint a negative portrait of Who God is and what we mean to Him.

In the very beginning the curtains were drawn back on the devil. He was revealed as a snake in the Garden of Eden where he spoke to Eve and spawned an improper picture of God's intent for mankind. He convinced Eve that God was selfish and was withholding all that was good for her life. Of course we are afforded insight into the scriptures and can see his spurious tales for what they really are—an attempt to instill fear and not faith in God's Word.

When we're presented with an adverse view of life, we must return to God's Word in order to make a paradigm shift. This means our perception becomes positive and our view is that of victory. It's through the Word of God we can receive His presence, rely on His promise and rehearse His performance. In essence, we get the picture.

Receive God's Presence

Having God's presence is profoundly important. Unfortunately, many people desire God's power and provision without having His presence. It's like the teenage boy who has just received his driver's license. This boy petitions for his father's car, asks for the car to be topped off with gas and even asks the father for spending money.

The father grants his son's request and then volunteers to join his son on the ride. However, the son rejects the father's presence because he is only interested in the father's possessions and provisions.

This gross neglect is perpetrated with many of God's people. If not careful, we can desire to have the King's ransom without having the King. In the presence of the Lord is the fullness of joy and at His right hand are pleasures evermore (Ps. 16:11). Jesus is not opposed to giving us blessings, but His presence should be considered optimum.

The main benefit of dwelling in the Lord's presence is the devil's absence. God's presence may not be seen, but it certainly is felt. His presence is like a strong wind. We cannot see it, but we definitely are able to see the effects of it. We may not see Jesus, but we feel His affect in our life immensely. When God steps on the scene, the devil has to flee.

To help lift the bands of segregation a federal Judge ordered the state of New Orleans to open its public schools to African-American children. White parents decided if black children were being let in, they would keep their children out.

The white parents threatened trouble if any black child attempted to attend their schools. The threats caused fear in many from the African-American community. As a result, many black parents decided to keep their children home. However, one six year old black girl attended the once segregated school.

Every day she walked to and from school through a heckling crowd. Both she and her parents walked with their heads up and their eyes straight ahead while two U.S. marshals walked in front and two behind them.

Later the six year old was interviewed by a local paper. The reporter asked the girl how she was able to walk to school through the taunting-angry mob. The child responded, "The presence of my parents and the marshals gave me courage."

Like this child, when we have the presence of our Lord we can walk through anything. Picture this and know the Lord's presence gives us strength to endure hardness.

Moses had the children of Israel ready to move forward and take the land God had promised. However, God was not pleased with Israel's disobedience. God told Moses they could advance, but not with His presence (Exo. 33:1-3). Wisely, Moses declined God's offer. Moses understood having a possession without God's presence could only provide a temporary pleasure.

Rely on God's Promise

> And the LORD answered me, and said, Write the vision, and make it plain upon tables, that he may run that readeth it.
>
> —Habakkuk 2:2

There is nothing more reliable than a promise from God. When we receive a promise from Him, we should feel fortunate. This world belongs to God and He oversees everything that takes place in it. Therefore, I am totally astonished to think that God would give any of us a promise. And yet He does.

By faith we must live off the promises of God. The Lord instructed Habakkuk to write the vision for the people and to make it plain. God's vision is equivalent to His promise. Once we're given God's vision we are instructed to run with it. The term "run with it" is the same as saying "live off the promise."

As a boy, one of my pastimes was riding my bike with the neighborhood guys. One day while riding I was hit by a car. The car's impact damaged my bike and left me lying on my back. I was immediately rushed to receive medical treatment.

The attending doctor informed my mother and me that my leg had been broken in two places. He further explained how he would have to set my leg in a cast. I was instructed not to apply any pressure to my leg for two months. After giving the negative news, the doctor looked me in the eyes and gave me a promise.

He said if I would adhere to his instructions, at the end of two months I would walk again, run again and above all, he promised I would be able to ride my bike again.

When I arrived home I received a lot of attention. My friends came over and tried to have a pity party for me. However, disappointment was not the order of the day. I began rehearsing what the doctor said to me. Rather than relishing in pity, I decided to rely on the doctor's promise. And just as he said, in two months I was walking, running and glory to God, riding my bike again.

The Lord wants us to live off His promise just as I relied on the promise of my physician. Oddly enough, we are able to live off physicians' promises without problems and they are only "practicing medicine." God is not practicing anything; He is the <u>Ancient of Days and the Great Physician.</u> There is nothing too hard for Him.

> The Lord is not slack concerning his promise, as some men count slackness; but is longsuffering to us-ward...
>
> —2nd Peter 3:9a

No matter what the enemy tries to show us by way of devastation or disappointment, we just need to get God's picture, and we can overcome any obstacle. God's friend Abraham had to learn how to live off the promises of God.

> And being not weak in faith, he considered not his own body now dead, when he was about an hundred years old, neither yet the deadness of Sarah's womb: He staggered not at the promise of God through unbelief; but was strong in faith, giving glory to God...
>
> —Romans 4:19-20

The Scripture conveys the Lord spoke to Abraham in a vision (Gen. 15:1). In other words, God gave Abraham a picture of his success. All Abraham had to do was believe and receive the promise. Now, for Abraham believing would prove to be difficult at first. Nevertheless, God would convince His friend by giving him a picture.

God promised Abraham that his generations would be incapable of being counted like the stars of heaven or the sand upon the seashore. In essence, God painted a picture for Abraham's success.

The unique thing about a promise is that we must wait for it until it manifests. Many become discouraged with God's promise because they are unwilling to be patient. However, those who wait will receive their reward.

> And let us not be weary in well doing: for in due season we shall reap, if we faint not.
>
> —Galatians 6:9

Rehearse God's Performance

> And being fully persuaded that, what he had promised, he was able also to perform.
>
> —Romans 4:21

Are you currently facing a problem with your finances, family or health? If so, do you find yourself worrying how you're going to overcome the predicament? Allow me to alleviate your stress. You will hurdle this current circumstance the same way you did the last—by the grace of God.

A well-known actor watched one of his movies for the first time with his six year old son. Once the movie had concluded the six year old with excitement asked, "Hey Dad, you know that thing in the movie where you swing from the rafters of that building? That's really cool, how did you do that?"

The actor said, "Well son, I didn't do that part...it was a stunt man." "What's a stunt man?" the boy asked. "That's someone who dresses like me and does things I can't do myself."

"Oh," he replied and walked out of the room looking a little confused. Later the boy asked, "Hey Dad, you know the part in the movie where you spin around on that gym bar and land on your feet? How did you do that?"

The actor responded, "Well, I didn't do that either. It was a gymnast double." "What's a gymnast double?" the son demanded. "That's a guy who dresses in my clothes and does the things I can't do." The father explained.

There was silence from the son, then he asked in a concerned voice, "Dad what did you do?" "I got all the glory," the father sheepishly replied.

That's how God's grace operates in our life. Jesus, by His death did what we could not do. Even now, we stand sheepishly as our God performs miracles in our lives.

The serpent's fear of what we see cannot affect us when we meditate on the way God performs. The children of Israel discovered this on their diaspora from Egypt. The Pharaoh and the army of Egypt pursued and cornered them by the Red Sea.

God commanded Moses to stretch forth his rod toward the sea and witness their salvation. Moses did as God commanded and the waters parted wide enough for the entire nation to cross over on dry land. When the last Jew made it through, the waters closed tighter than a zipper. The Egyptian army was swallowed by the crashing waves and drowned.

The devil may try to pursue you with the pains of your past. He will attempt to discourage you with negative images. In fact, you may be facing a difficult situation right now. Whatever you do don't give up just look up and see the picture of your God performing on your behalf.

The Bible tells of Daniel who prayed to God out of his sufferings and waited patiently for God's answer. Amazingly, the first day Daniel prayed, the Lord sent an angel. However, the angel had to fight in the spiritual realm (Dan. 10:12-13). When the angel finally arrived, he literally gave Daniel his picture of victory.

Another powerful depiction of the importance of rehearsing God's performance is captured in the book of Second Chronicles. Jehoshaphat and all of Judah were surrounded by formidable foes. At first Judah was shaking like a dryer on the spin cycle. Jehoshaphat gathered the people in order to corral their attention on God and not their circumstance.

With passion Jehoshaphat rehearsed Who God was and what He had done (2nd Chron. 20:6-7). By rehearsing the bigness of God, Jehoshaphat reduced the bigness of their predicament. Sometimes we become overwhelmed by situations and go to God as if it's too great for Him to handle. Fact is, after we tell God about the bigness of our problem; we must turn to our problem and tell it about the bigness of our God.

We must see every problem as an opportunity for God to perform a miracle. Many Christians complain today about not seeing the miracles of God. Oddly enough, God's hands are tied because some of those same people give up too soon. They give in to the serpent's fear of what they see rather than allowing God to give them a picture for their finances, family, health or anything that matters.

You can untie the hands of God when you have faith in His Word. Through faith you can unleash God's power to perform in every area of your life.

> Then said the LORD unto me, thou hast well seen: for I will hasten my word to perform it.
>
> —Jeremiah 1:12

God will grant you His presence, promise and performance. This is what He desires to do. However, there is something you must do which allows God to prevail and the devil (the serpent) to fail. You must see yourself the way God sees you—the lender not the borrower, the head not the tail, above only and not beneath. Is this what you want? If so, "get the picture."

Chapter Thirteen
Overcoming the Fear of the Dragon
"Addressing the Spirit of Paranoia"

> And among these nations shalt thou find no ease, neither shall the sole of thy foot have rest: but the LORD shall give thee there a *trembling heart*, and *failing of eyes*, and *sorrow of mind*: And thy life shall hang in doubt before thee; and thou shalt fear day and night, and shalt have none assurance of thy life: In the morning thou shalt say, Would God it were even! and at even thou shalt say, Would God it were morning! for the fear of thine heart wherewith thou shalt fear, and for the sight of thine eyes which thou shalt see.
>
> —Deuteronomy 28:65-67

The consequences for disobeying God's Word are the fear of the lion, serpent and the dragon. These fears describe the state of the world. These same fears are also mentioned in the book of Psalm.

Psalm 91:13 depicts three metaphors that illustrate how Satan brings fear to people: the lion, the adder (serpent) and the dragon.

> Thou shall tread upon the *lion* and *adder*: the young lion and the *dragon* shalt thou trample under feet.
>
> —Psalm 91:13

The opening passage speaks of a trembling heart. This describes the lion's fear of what we hear. It's when Satan brings fear by way of negative words. But Psalm 112:7 speaks of not being afraid of evil tidings or bad news, because our hearts are fixed, trusting in the Lord.

The passage also speaks of the failing of eyes. That's the serpent's fear of what we see. Proverbs 3:25 calls it sudden fear. In times like these we must look unto Jesus. We must look toward heaven and get the vision God has for our life. We must learn to see things that are not seen, to walk by faith and not by sight. Our eyes fail when we're looking at the wrong thing.

Lastly, the passage talks about sorrow of mind. This describes how Satan plays games with our minds. He defeats a Christian first and foremost in the mind. If he can control our thought-life he'll control our life; for as a man thinketh in his heart, so is he. If he can give us the wrong perception about God and what God has for our life, he can manipulate, intimidate and eventually dominate us.

BREAK THE POWER OF MANIPULATION

 For God hath not given us the spirit of fear; but of power, and of love, and of a sound mind.

> —2nd Timothy 1:7

The preceding scripture speaks directly to the dragon's fear. The dragon's fear is synonymous with the term stronghold. A stronghold is a system of thinking that formulates a belief that's not based on the truth. A stronghold can contribute to having a spirit of fear.

All three terms are synonymous, but for now we use the term dragon's fear. In order to fully comprehend the dragon's fear, permit the following explanation. By definition a dragon is considered a huge snake. However, a dragon is more commonly known as a mythological sea monster or primeval creature of chaos. In essence, the dragon's fear is a fear that really does not exist.

Those who are vexed with the dragon's fear are forced into a system of manipulation. The devil is able to manipulate them by playing with their mind (2nd Timothy 1:7 reveals God does not give us a spirit of fear (dragon's fear). In contrast, He gives us His love and a sound mind.

Once we truly comprehend the breadth, width, depth and height of God's love for us our minds will be sound. Having a sound mind means we are secure in knowing the Lord protects us from every plan of the enemy.

The very spirit of manipulation is to control through burdening the mind. Our enemy is the devil and he looks to manipulate us with disturbing thoughts. Some suffer from what is called nervous break-downs. These break-downs can cause headaches and delusional disturbances. In essence, the devil uses deceit to alter our state of mind from love and trust to suspicion and fear.

In the first book of the Bible, the devil is depicted as a serpent (Gen. 3:1). Moreover, in the final book of the Bible the devil is depicted as a dragon (Rev. 12:9). The question becomes which is he? Well, the answer is discovered in the book of John 8:44. We are told that Satan is not only a liar, but he's the father of lies.

Having this truth revealed should prepare us for the devil's plot. The devil seeks to instill fear of all sorts. He will bring the fear of the lion (fears we hear) and the fear of the *did God really say...*

serpent (fears we see), but ultimately he looks to manipulate our lives through the dragon's fear (fears that don't exist).

non-capital

We are especially vulnerable to the devil's manipulation when we try to overcome various challenges in life through our own power. I read an analogy that expresses this very concept. The analogy conveyed how portable camcorders have a battery pack for power.

Instructions typically recommend that users allow the battery pack to completely discharge before recharging, especially the first few times it's used. This actually increases the endurance of the battery.

In like manner, our trials "discharge" us, emptying us of our dependence on human strength and increasing our capacity to receive God's limitless power.

★ When we rely totally on the Lord and trust Him, He protects us from any manipulation the enemy may design for our demise.

Break the Power of Intimidation

The dragon's fear could be considered the deadliest of all fears, because it will keep us in a state of panic. A perpetual state of panic is considered paranoia. Paranoia is to the child of God what kryptonite is to Superman.

Paranoia is characterized chiefly by delusions of persecution. Also there's a tendency on the part of the individual to be suspicious and distrustful of others. This described paranoia is what I refer to as the dragon's fear. Again, God has not given us a spirit of fear — the dragon's fear. God has given us His Spirit of love, wisdom and a sound mind.

God desires that we live uninhibited. Through our faith in Jesus we are capable of accomplishing all things. However, when we are burdened by paranoia our lives become restricted and we focus on defeat rather than victory.

The devil's strategy is to progress from manipulation to intimidation, and from paranoia to paralysis. When our movement is impaired, we are stifled in our spiritual walk. God created us to have dominion and subdue the entire earth. However, the dragon's fear makes us timid and afraid of our own shadow.

It's not enough for God to give us His Spirit; we must willingly receive His Spirit. We receive His Spirit to stand against Satan and his seductive powers. The world we live in is heavily influenced with satanic spirits.

> For we wrestle not against flesh and blood, but against principalities, against powers, against the rulers of the darkness of this world, against spiritual wickedness in high places.
>
> —Ephesians 6:12

These wicked spirits try to place fear in us for the purpose of causing intimidation. The aforementioned passage states for we wrestle not against flesh and blood, but take note, it doesn't convey that we don't wrestle. Many of God's people complain because they have to fight. They are intimidated and look to avoid confrontation with the enemy at all cost.

God promised Israel a land in which they would grow and prosper. Israel was excited concerning God's Promised Land and they journeyed far to receive it. Upon reaching their destination they discovered the land was occupied by giant men. At this point, the dragon's fear entered into their hearts and took control of their minds.

Israel began complaining to Moses. They assumed the worse and imagined defeat. In fact, two and a half tribes decided to settle for less than God's best when it came to possessing the land (Num. 32:1-33). Moses allowed them to stop short of their promised possession, but he still commanded them to go and fight with their brothers for their land.

I ask you, are you willing to settle for less than God's best for your life? Are you going to allow the dragon's fear to intimidate you? The truth is this; God doesn't want us intimidated. God will place us in situations that provoke courage in us.

> Have not I commanded thee? Be strong and of a good courage; be not afraid, neither be thou dismayed: for the LORD thy God is with thee, whithersoever thou goest.
>
> —Joshua 1:9

Amen!

I can recall a time when my son was being bullied by one of the neighborhood boys. The matter had gotten really out of hand. My son was perpetually late coming home from school because he was forced to take a circuitous route in order to elude this nuisance.

Finally, I personally took my son to the corner where this bully hung-out. I realize this was not the best course of action, but I was looking to give him a class on courage not ethics.

Although he was afraid, I encouraged my son to confront this bully. Above all, I reminded him that I was there as his protection. Well, he confronted the bully and stood his ground. In the end, he earned respect from that bully and got rid of his fears.

> Stand therefore, having your loins girt about with truth, and having on the breastplate of righteousness; And your feet shod with the preparation of the gospel of peace; Above all, taking the shield of faith, wherewith ye shall be able to quench all the fiery darts of the wicked. And take the helmet of salvation, and the sword of the Spirit, which is the word of God.
>
> —Ephesians 6:14-17

This is what Jesus does for us. He walks with us through our valleys and He gives us strength to confront the enemy in battle. And if by chance we are intimidated, His Spirit is there to encourage us to stand.

Break the Power of Domination

The dragon's fear is used to bring us under the devil's manipulation and intimidation, just so he can dominate us. Through domination the devil is able to direct our movement. Remember that two and a half tribes of Israel stopped short of their God-given destiny. This is because they allowed their fear to direct them and not God's Spirit.

There are people who are agoraphobic. They are afraid of public places because they fear crowds. This fear has placed restrictions on their life. God's Spirit leads us to help people not avoid them. If the devil can direct our movement eventually he can cause us to neglect our God-given duty.

Let's consider Jacob's account. His very name revealed his early nature (he supplants). At the time of his birth he grabbed hold of his twin brother Esau's heel attempting to emerge from the womb first. Later in his life he continued to take hold of the possessions of other's—his brother's birthright—his father's blessings—his uncle's flock.

After tricking his father to receive the birthright, Jacob found himself face-to-face with a cantankerous Esau. Their confrontation ended with Jacob being verbally threatened. In fear for his life Jacob fled his brother's wrath.

Through Esau's threats the devil was able to dominate and change the course of Jacob's life. However, while on the run Jacob encountered the Lord's presence. The Lord spoke to Jacob in a dream to give him divine direction (Gen. 28:12-15).

Jacob lived for years as a fugitive with his uncle Laban. After 20 years, two wives and over a dozen children, Jacob decided to journey back to the land God had promised him. However, he was now tormented with the dragon's fear. Jacob feared his brother's wrath and imagined the worse. He divided his family into bands and had them wait for what he thought was pending doom.

If not put in check, the dragon's fear of paranoia can divide homes. It can cause us to move in a direction that God has not ordered. And the devil will play with our emotions like a puppet.

While preparing for a reunion with his brother, in whom he still dreadfully feared; Jacob was visited in the night by the Lord (Gen. 32:7-30). Once again the Lord gave Jacob's life direction by changing his name. Jacob's new name literally gave him a new nature.

Soon after, Jacob discovered his fears were unwarranted, because Esau greeted him with endearment. The dragon's fear caused Jacob to perceive his brother as a foe when in fact Esau was his friend. Truth is Jacob feared the uncertainty of his brother's love.

Jacob allowed the devil to dominate his direction in life through the dragon's fear. However, God was able to break that spirit of domination by reassuring Jacob of His divine presence.

A spy was captured and sentenced to death by a general in the Persian army. This general had the strange custom of giving condemned criminals a choice between the firing squad and "the big, black door."

The moment for execution drew near, and guards brought the spy to the Persian general. "What will it be," asked the general, "The firing squad or 'the big, black door?'" the spy hesitated for a long time. Finally he chose the firing squad.

A few minutes later, hearing the shots ring out confirming the spy's execution, the general turned to his aide and said, "They always prefer the known to the unknown. People fear what they don't know. Yet, we gave him a choice."

"What lies beyond the big door?" asked the aide. "Freedom," replied the general. "I've known only a few brave enough to take that door."

Beloved, the devil will try to dominate us with the fear of the unknown, but we can combat the unknown with what we do know. We know that God is more powerful than the devil and we know He longs to show us His love.

If the fear of the dragon has gotten a grip on your life, break the stronghold of manipulation, intimidation and domination.

Addressing the dragon's fear is only the beginning. To truly gain the victory, we must eliminate it entirely.

Chapter Fourteen
Eliminating the Spirit of Paranoia

> **There were they in great fear, where no fear was**: for God hath scattered the bones of him that encampeth against thee: thou hast put them to shame, because God hath despised them.
>
> —Psalm 53:5

The opening scripture describes the very concept of the dragon's fear. It reads some were in a state of fear where there was no reason to fear. This described state of fear is considered paranoia.

For those who are plagued with paranoia addressing it can be a prodigious task. Even so, addressing it is only part of the solution. To rid ourselves of paranoia altogether we must put a three-step process into practice.

This process is not always simple, yet and still, when practiced the results can be quite liberating. To eliminate the dragon's fear, we must face it—trace it—and erase it by replacing it.

Facing the Dragon's Fear

> But the *fearful*, and unbelieving, and the abominable, and murderers, and whoremongers, and sorcerers, and idolaters, and all liars, shall have their part in the lake which burneth with fire and brimstone: which is the second death.
>
> —Revelation 21:8

The aforementioned passage chronicles those who have transgressed against God. These transgressors will have a future in eternal fire. Most interesting, the fearful transgressor stands at the top of the list.

This term fearful derives from the Greek word Deilos which means cowardly. Through further examination of this word we discover it's the kind of fear that causes us to lose our moral gumption. We no longer consider what's right and tragically we are hindered from following God.

God pronounced His power, provisions and peace over man (Gen. 1:28). However, the devil arrived on the scene with implications that God was malicious and manipulating. He insidiously instilled the dragon's fear in Eve. Man was given power by God to exercise dominion over all the animals and to subdue the earth. Nevertheless, the devil suggested God was mean because He did not allow them to partake of every tree in the Garden. Then he purported God was a liar because He promised death as a consequence of disobedience (Gen. 3:1-5). As a result of listening to the devil's claims fear entered the hearts of Adam and Eve.

They felt they were missing out on the good things. That which was deemed off-limits was touched. They failed to see behind the enemies plot. The devil knew God provided Adam and Eve with a wonderful life, and that His grace and favor was extended to them. Their luxury was made possible because of God's love.

117

God's love affords us the kind of life we don't deserve. His love is a garden that allows us to grow and blossom into the creatures He designed us to become. His Word is like nutrients that stimulate growth and pesticides that ward off the enemies influence.

> There is no fear in love; but perfect love casteth out fear: because fear hath torment. He that feareth is not made perfect in love.
>
> — 1st John 4:18

The only way the devil can penetrate the power of God's love is to get us to distrust and disobey God's Word. Therefore, he spawned lies to Eve and she shared them with Adam. As a result, they were snared by the dragon's fear of what's not there. They believed the wrath of God prevailed over the love of God.

In haste they covered themselves in fig leaves. A figurative interpretation of the fig here is Fear In God. In essence, they lived their life in constant fear that God was out to harm them. Therefore, they hid themselves from the presence of God (Gen. 3:8).

Tragically the dragon's fear hinders us from following God. We may even attempt to hide ourselves from God's presence. Fortunately for us, there is nowhere we can hide from the out-stretched arm of God. David discovered this very fact and wrote:

> Whither shall I go from thy spirit? Or wither shall I flee from thy presence? If I ascend up into heaven, thou art there: if I make my bed in hell, behold, thou art there. If I take the wings of the morning, and dwell in the uttermost parts of the sea; Even there shall thy hand lead me, and thy right hand shall hold me.
>
> — Psalm 139:8-10

The proper response to the dragon's fear is first and foremost facing it. Because of this fear Adam and Eve thought the worst of God. It gripped their hearts and threatened to take control of their lives. A crooked morality distorted their reality.

Therefore, God caused them to face their fear by asking Adam a profound question—"*Where are you?*" Recognizing where we are and facing it allows us to make positive strides toward breaking the devil's grip and returning to the Father's grace.

This also ushers us into tracing where the dragon's fear began.

Tracing the Dragon's Fear

Adam faced his fear by openly admitting that he was fearful (Gen. 3:10) because he was nude. The word nude means devoid of covering; it also denotes lacking some consideration and unsupported. We can deduce that he somehow realized through his state of nudity he had lost his covering. Therefore, this disobedience that brought about the dragon's fear in their lives opened the door to feelings of un-acceptance.

Although the scripture reveals their eyes were opened (Gen.3:7), somehow their senses became dull to the love of God. A foundation of love and faith was replaced by inadequacy and fear.

God gave Adam and Eve His blessings. He pronounced they would reign and rule; they would multiply and have meaning. He designed and desired for them to have creative order. It was His volition that they had victory and He predestined them to prosper.

With all of this going for them, how did God's plans for Adam and Eve go awry? The simple fact is they gave credence to the wrong voice. They allowed the devil's voice to supersede the voice of God. Where God spoke prosperity the devil spoke problems. When God spoke superiority the devil spoke suspicion.

Many of God's people suffer from the fear of inadequacy. For as long as they can remember they were told they would not succeed. However, the devil is a liar! God created all of us to succeed.

> I will praise thee; for I am fearfully and wonderfully made: marvellous are thy works; and that my soul knoweth right well. My substance was not hid from thee, when I was made in secret, and curiously wrought in the lowest parts of the earth. Thine eyes did see my substance, yet being unperfect; and in thy book all my members were written, which in continuance were fashioned, when as yet there was none of them. How precious also are thy thoughts unto me, O God! how great is the sum of them!
>
> —Psalm 139:14-17

The passage above conveys just how much God loves us. Through His abiding love He fashions us with precision and He's acquainted with everything that makes us who we are. God does not place His quality time into people with no purpose. He did not fashion us for failure. The Lord is preparing us for great things! His thoughts toward us are thoughts of good and not evil (Jer. 29:11). He wants to grant us a future laced with His favor so we may abound in every good work.

A medieval fletcher held a peculiar job. His vocation was to handcraft arrows for the archer's use. The fletcher would start by choosing his tree wisely. He desired the kind of wood that was tuff and sturdy.

After selection of the proper wood the fletcher would remove all knots. Once the knots were removed the fletcher strategically placed feathers at the end of the arrow. Removing the knots and adding the feathers was imperative to ensure an arrow was capable of hitting its target.

God like a fletcher created us to hit our target. He did not design us to move aimlessly in life missing the mark. He is firmly holding us in His hand and with precision He is removing the "Nots" out of us. Some may have said you were "not" smart enough—"not" strong enough—"not" important enough. If so, God wants you to trace those "nots" so He can remove them.

God needed Adam to trace the source of his negative information. Therefore, God asked the question—"Who told thee you were naked?"

You see, our confession is a result of our belief. Our belief is a result of our thinking. Our thinking comes as a result of our knowledge. Finally, our knowledge is a result of our source and there are only two sources in this world—the devil and God. The one with the greater voice will determine whether we are plagued with the dragon's fear or not.

> Therefore take no thought, *saying*, What shall we eat? Or, What shall we drink? Or, Wherewithal shall we be clothed?
>
> —Matthew 6:31

In the previous scripture Jesus commanded us concerning our phobias. More importantly, He gave insight as to how we succumb to anxieties. Jesus said take no thought from the negative source by speaking the negative circumstance.

When we trace an adverse situation in our life, we'll discover its origin was negative words that were spoken. God will remove those "nots" that hold us back from hitting the target of success. He will use each negative word that was spoken to elevate us to our next level. Albeit, we must give His voice and make His Word final authority. Amen!

And unto Adam he said, **Because thou hast hearkened unto the voice of thy wife**, and hast eaten of the tree, of which I commanded thee, saying, Thou shalt not eat of it: cursed is the ground for thy sake; in sorrow shalt thou eat of it all the days of thy life...

—Genesis 3:17

Listening to the wrong voice can cause us pain. However, once we trust God totally and follow Him whole heartedly, He will erase the dragon's fear by replacing it with His love.

Erase and Replace the Dragon's Fear

Unto Adam also and to his wife did the Lord God make coats of skins, and clothed them.

—Genesis 3:21

I'm elated to report Adam and Eve's story didn't conclude with the devil getting the victory. Ultimately, the devil desired to separate this couple from the love of the Father. They certainly thought their actions drove a permanent wedge between them and God.

After their disobedience to the word of God, Adam and Eve discovered their nakedness. They felt they were without the support of God. In contrast, the Lord never left them and to signify this very fact He covered this couple with coats of skin.

This skin would serve as a symbol of Jesus Who would later redeem humanity (another story for another time). The important thing to take away is the Lord erased their fear by replacing what they thought they loss—His covering.

This singular act was pivotal in eliminating the fear of the dragon. There will be times when we all come short of making the grade. We all have sinned and come short of God's glory. One of the greatest sins we can commit is the sin of fearfulness. I say this not because it's the worst of all sins. I say this because this sin can be considered the gateway to other sins.

NOTE / SUMMARY!
When we are full of fear it means we lack faith. It's only through faith that we can follow God. The Just live by faith (Rom. 1:17), walk by faith (2nd Cor. 5:7) and fight the good fight of faith (1st Tim. 6:12).

Sin separates us from God and living in a perpetual state of fear is sin. If you find yourself engulfed in the sin of fear don't lose heart, because God has a life preserver and it's His love.

> Above all, love each other deeply, because love covers over a multitude of sins.
> —1st Peter 4:8 niv

Once we fully appreciate God's love, all our fears will be erased. If we focus on our failures the dragon's fear appears. Adam and Eve fell because fear entered their hearts and they distrusted God. There's a propensity for us to view every situation in a negative way. Therefore, our recollection of Adam and Eve's account is called the "Fall." However, if they were here to give their testimony I dare to say rather than focusing on how they fell, they might testify how God picked them up.

A world renowned composer was being interviewed by a television reporter. In the interview the reporter asked the composer, "Is there any question you've never been asked that you would like someone to ask you?"

"Well, yes, there is one," he replied. "What do you think of the many songs you've written that did not become hits?' My reply would be I still think they were wonderful."

God, too, has an unshakeable delight in what—and whom—he has made. He thinks each of His children is wonderful. Whether we're a "hit" in the eyes of others or not, He will always think we're wonderful and cover us with His love.

Adam and Eve discovered first-hand the love of God. Sure they made a major mistake. They allowed the voice of the enemy to come between them and the One Who adored them vehemently.

The devil told them they were "not" worthy of receiving God's very best. He said they were "not" worthy of being beloved by God. But God unraveled the devil's "nots" and revealed His love. While the devil badgers us with the issue of unworthiness, God steps in with the issue of worth. None of us deserve God's love, but all of us have been given the opportunity to receive it.

God's love is precious and priceless. It can never be purchased, He freely gives it away. Don't waste time pondering if you are worthy of the Father's love. Just receive the fact that you are worth it.

When we are able to face any fear, trace its source, and erase our fear by replacing it with the love of God, the dragon's fear of paranoia will truly be eliminated. AMEN!

No matter what happens in life, remember, God has you covered.

Chapter Fifteen

The Disrespect of Fear

But without faith it is impossible to please him: for he that cometh to God must believe that he is, and that he is a rewarder of them that diligently seek him.

—Hebrews 11:6

A man sat in his study diligently reviewing some plans for work when he was abruptly disturbed by a loud sound. Upon investigating he discovered it was noise from the television show his son was watching in the next room. He asked his son to turn the television's volume down.

His request was met with a negative response from his son. Surprised, the father entered the room where the son was seated and issued this admonishment: "Son, your being upset changes nothing around here. However, if I'm upset, your whole world can change in an instant. Therefore, it behooves you to make sure that your attitude does not upset me."

On that same token, we please God with our faith. It's gratifying to know we have the capability to please Him. What's even more rewarding is to know we don't have to perform outstanding exploits to do so. Since we know our faith pleases our Lord it would be to our benefit to remain in faith.

The converse of faith is fear and the consequence of fear is the Father's displeasure. Through fear we also disrespect Him. Imagine that! We can disrespect God when we remain in fear.

When we have respect for someone we give them our regards or consideration. In other words, they have our undivided attention. Above all, the Lord deserves our respect. Nothing in this world should command our attention more than God Himself. No matter what, Jesus should be the center and circumference, base and boundary, balance and beauty and the sum and substance of our entire life.

> **Looking unto Jesus** the author and finisher of our faith…**For consider him** that endured such contradiction of sinners against himself, lest ye be wearied and faint in your minds.
>
> —Hebrews 12:2-3

The Scripture conveys we ought to be "looking" unto Jesus. It's interesting to note it did not simply say look at Jesus rather it stresses "looking." With the suffix "ing" added to the word look, it commands us not to just take a look at Jesus, but to keep our focus on Him.

We offer the Lord our sincere respect by focusing on Him. However, when the vicissitudes of this world pull our attention in the opposite direction we move from showing Him respect to disrespect. No matter how you slice it, perpetual fear shows God disrespect.

No Born-again Believer desires to disrespect God, but it happens if they're operating in perpetual fear. There's an acronym that delineates fear for us and it depicts the actions taken when we give place to fear. Fear can be acrostically understood as:

Forgets the greatness of your God

Envisions the worst

Accepts defeat before the fight

Rejects God's way of deliverance

Forgets the Greatness of Your God

> Great is the LORD, and greatly to be praised; and his greatness is unsearchable.
>
> —Psalm 145:3

The last thing we ever want to do is forget that our God is great. Nevertheless, this is the first effect of fear. Fear causes us to have spiritual amnesia. When we ought to be praising God for his awesome splendor fear creates just the opposite response. Through fear we go to God quivering for answers to life's problems.

Whether it's a challenge in our marriage, with our children, our health, our finances, fear says, "How will you get through this predicament?" Faith speaks differently. Faith reminds us in every situation the Answer to life's difficulties is Jesus.

If you're facing a problem right now and you're wondering how you're going to get out of it, let me remind you. You'll recover from this problem the way you have recovered in the past—with God's help. The question should never be, "How can I get out of this predicament?" Rather we should ask, "What will God get out of this predicament?"

We must never forget God remains in control even when our world appears to be spinning out of control. Israel was given commandment to teach their future generations about God's exploits. This mandate was put in place to safeguard against them forgetting God's power over their problems.

> That they might set their hope in God, and **not forget the works of God**, but keep his commandments
> —Psalm 78:7

In spite of the fact that God worked many miracles, Israel still forgot about His power. They forgot how God delivered them from the mistreatment of the Egyptians. They forgot how God led them with a cloud by day and His fire at night. As soon as they felt hunger pangs, they wondered if God could satisfy their appetites.

> And they tempted God in their heart by asking meat for their lust. Yea, **they spake against God**; they said, **Can God** furnish a table in the wilderness?
> —Psalm 78:18-19

Israel allowed their hunger for meat to displace their honor for the Master. Through the fear of not having enough to eat they disrespected God. In fact, the scripture above reveals they spoke against God by saying, "Can God provide food in the wilderness?"

They took their eyes off of God and focused more on their issue. By magnifying the problem they were forced to ask, *"Can God?"* However, had they magnified the Lord in the midst of their problem they would have concluded, *"God can!"* Amazingly, the proper order of two words can change our predicament from bitter to better, and can transform us from the gutter-most to the uttermost.

> How oft did they provoke him in the wilderness, and grieve him in the desert! Yea, they turned back and tempted God, and **limited the Holy One of Israel**.
> —Psalm 78:40-41

Israel limited God from operating on their behalf through fear, doubt and unbelief. In contrast, faith releases the power of God in our lives. Through faith the crooked paths are made straight and stumbling blocks become stepping stones.

ENVISIONS THE WORST

Perception is vital when it comes to gaining the victory. Even in our darkest hour if we can envision the best, success is within our grasp.

The actor Jamie Foxx did a superb job at playing Ray Charles in the movie, "Ray." There was one moment in the movie that was pivotal to Ray Charles' success. This was the moment when a young Ray Charles completely loss his eyesight.

Ray's mother was left with the task of getting her young son oriented to life as a blind person. As Ray stumbled and fumbled his way around their old cabin he found himself quite discouraged having no sight. He sat down in despair and began crying out to his mother for help.

At that moment Ray's mother decided not to hold his hand and lead him around. She commanded Ray to get up and she told him, "Just because you're blind it doesn't mean you can't see." His mother knew Ray lost his vision, but she wanted to instill within him the possibility to envision. This mother knew if her son saw himself as helpless he would be helpless. However, if Ray could envision success in his darkest moment the possibility of success would be within his grasp.

Giving into our fears only causes us to envision the worst case scenarios. Consider the child who cries out for his parents in the dark. This child sees the proverbial Boogeyman only because in the dark he envisions the worst. Interestingly, the Boogeyman never manifests in the light.

Beloved, God knows if you would just envision the best for your life in spite of what's happening the best will eventually become your reality. Think with me, the same mental energy it takes to envision the worst can be spent on envisioning the best. Fear will always cause us to see the worst in every situation. This is why it's paramount we remain in faith.

Faith is our catalyst to receiving our Canaan. In this instance Canaan represents God's promise. The Lord promised Israel a land for their inheritance that would flow with milk and honey (Exo. 3:8). In essence, God proclaimed His favor on this real-estate. All Israel had to do was follow God's lead and walk into their blessing. Albeit, one thing made the transition more complicated than it had to be—Israel envisioned the worst.

Upon reaching their divine destiny, Israel pictured themselves too weak to take what God proclaimed was rightfully theirs.

> And there we saw the giants, the sons of Anak, which come of the giants: and **we were in our own sight as grasshoppers**, and so we were in their sight.
> —Numbers 13:33

Israel held a distorted view of themselves and it caused them to disobey God. They disrespected God by considering the giant's power over His. However, we can't be too hard on Israel; after all, they had just spent 400 years under Egypt's oppression, right? 400 years of being told you were worthless and then suddenly catapulted into battle would place fear in anyone, right?

Sorry! God accepts no excuses, not when He's the One giving us strength for any battle. God used frogs to pry Israel from Pharaoh's greedy grip (Exo. 8:2). Surely He could use Israel (even as grasshoppers) to dislodge the inhabitants of Canaan.

Listen! Don't allow someone else to possess the promise the Lord gave you. Even if you see yourself as a grasshopper get what God has for you. The key to living life without limitations is not how you see yourself, but how you see your God. Begin envisioning the best not the worst and by faith claim victory in every area of your life.

Accepts Defeat before the Fight

> Wherefore take unto you the whole armour of God, that ye may be able to withstand in the evil day, and having done all, to stand. Stand...
>
> —Ephesians 6:13-14

Life delivers a series of blows and recovery can be difficult. Fear will cause us to throw in the towel too soon. However, the command of God is simple and definitive. If your career collapses, the economy collides with catastrophe, or your foundation crumbles, God with authority thunders this word –Stand!

If the devil threatens to take your health, home and dismember your household the operative command is "Stand!" Truth is we all must fight whether we like it or not. However, the question becomes is there anything worth fighting for? Yes, your health, home, and household are worth fighting for; and more importantly, God's will is worth the fight, so stand!

It takes courage to stand. Please don't misinterpret the true meaning of courage. Courage is not the absence of fear; courage is action in the face of fear. We all have moments when fear visits our doorstep. However, when fear comes knocking at your door allow Jesus to answer. The Bible says He's in us and is greater than anything we will face in this world (1st John 4:4).

The devil loves to sell wolf tickets. If allowed he'll purport himself to be big and bad. Jesus called satan the prince of this world (John 14:30). This is why there is so much hell on earth.

A third grade teacher was covering the different shapes of objects with her class. The teacher gave examples of objects like triangle shapes as well as squares. Then she asked the class, "What shape is the world?" From the back of the class a boy raised his hand. Once called upon the boy answered, "Last night my father was watching the evening news and he said, 'The world is in baaad shape.'"

Although the world is in bad shape we serve the God of creation. He can fashion and form your world. He can give water to the places that are dry and provide light to the places that are dark. When everything seems to be breaking down our God provides our breakthrough. Victory is ours if we don't accept defeat.

God appeared to Moses of all places in the desert. This was a dry place, a time when it seemed nothing significant would occur. Moses had retreated in seclusion from the Pharaoh's wrath. The very person Moses cowered from, God told him to confront (Exo. 3:10).

After the Lord provided Moses with the assignment to speak to Pharaoh, Moses complained of his stuttering in order to avoid the task. Moses' fear caused him to accept defeat before the fight.

At this point, God gave Moses a class on courage (Exo. 4:1-9). The Lord displayed signs unto Moses. These signs were significant in that they were designed to give Moses faith in God's ability to succeed over Moses' inability to fail. The Lord taught Moses concerning His power to perform. God was replacing Moses' fear with faith.

Like Moses, you may think that problem is too big to confront. However, I want you to know that issue has been bothering you far too long. God is ready to provide water where it's dry and light where it's dark. Don't accept defeat before the fight because you'll rob yourself of the victorious life.

Rejects God's Way of Deliverance

> There is no fear in love; but perfect love casteth out fear: because fear hath torment. He that feareth is not made perfect in love. We love him, because he first loved us.
>
> —1st John 4:18-19

Jesus is the Answer to a fearless life. He is God's love personified. This is important to know because this world is saturated with fear. Fear is everywhere! To live the kind of life God intended and created us to live we must get beyond this world's grip. And the grip of this world is fear.

We can break the world's negative gravitational pull by receiving God's love. According to the Scripture, God so loved the world He gave His Son Jesus (John 3:16). In essence, God knew that our world needed His love and the best way to display His love was through Jesus.

This world is fractured, flawed and failing. The only escape from definite defeat is to receive Jesus and to become developed in His nature. The nature of Jesus Christ is love. Without the love of Christ permeating in our hearts we'll experience defeat in every area of our lives.

Unfortunately, many people are suffering because they reject God's way of deliverance. They allow fear to dictate the terms. Relationships falter and lives are left in shambles due to rejecting God's love and giving into the world's lust.

A man and his wife sought marital counseling from their pastor. After the pastor heard their situation he concluded by saying, "You can recover from hurts and heal from pain if you'll love one another."

The husband then complained, "We can't agree on anything!" To this the pastor admonished, "The Bible commands you to love your wife." The man inserted, "I don't see her as my wife." The pastor added, "The Bible says love your neighbor." The man objected, "I don't see her as my neighbor." Finally, the pastor warned, "The Bible says love your enemy." Stifled, the husband said, "Well, I guess I have no excuse."

Beloved, when it comes to God's love we are left without excuse. We must develop in the love of God then we will receive our deliverance. Remember, after the Lord saves us, there cannot be any authentic deliverance without actual development. After all, God expects nothing less from His people than the desire to develop in His love.

It's not difficult to love like God when we concentrate on the fact that He loved us first (1st John 4:19). Therefore, live your life like God loves you. This simple and yet profound concept is critical to a life filled with faith not fear.

When Jesus revealed He was the One Whom God sent to save humanity, He was rejected. Jesus was God's way of deliverance then and He is God's way of deliverance now. For that reason, we must accept God's way through expressing Jesus' life, light and love.

Every morning when you wake up, get up! When you get up, go down (in worship) so when you go out you can face a negative world with God's nature of love. Our love must manifest in the concrete not just hover somewhere in the abstract.

Remember, fear keeps us from loving like God; fear robs us of the opportunity of living a life without limitations; fear embodies negative forces which work against God's favor in our lives; fear causes us to forget our God is great; fear makes us envision the worst of any situation; fear drives us to accept defeat before God can grant us victory; and above all, fear causes us to reject God's way of deliverance.

Remarkably, in a world full of fear we can choose to be fearless. <u>All forms of fear are dispelled through love</u>. Therefore, <u>we must live our lives knowing our God loves us, and we reciprocate His love by loving others because He loves us all.</u>

We are God's treasured possessions and for that reason He desires the kind of life that reflects His goodness, favor and His love for all of us. This life is obtained only through faith in Jesus Christ—It's all about Him!

Notes

Notes

Notes

Notes

Notes

Notes